DEDICATION

This special printing of SUCCESSFUL COIN HUNTING is dedicated to KELLYCO METAL DETECTOR DISTRIBUTORS and the world famous KELLYCO TEST TEAM.

KELLYCO METAL DETECTOR DISTRIBUTORS is one of the oldest and finest companies in the field of metal detecting. A company outstanding in their unselfish dedication and service to the hobby of coin, relic and treasure hunting. Quick to donate time, money and resources to the advancement of detecting, KELLYCO has pioneered new ways to assist the newcomer to understand and use their detector for the deepest and most efficient searching for coins and buried treasure.

Stu Auerbach, President of KELLYCO, a well known coin and treasure hunter has traveled throughout the United States and the world recovering old coins and buried treasure. In his thirty years of metal detecting, Stu has always made it a point to take the time to sit down with government officials to explain what metal detectors do and who the typical users are of this equipment. Through his individual efforts many countries now allow the use of metal detectors where before, permission could NOT have been obtained. Vacationers and travelers can now carry their detectors with them and enhance their searching for that hidden "Treasure Trove" thanks to Stu Auerbach and KELLYCO METAL DETECTOR DISTRIBUTORS.

The KELLYCO TEST TEAM, financed through KELLYCO and is in no way connected to any manufacturer, independently tests metal detectors under actual field conditions. This special team is made up of experienced detector users who have attended educational seminars sponsored by Garrett Electronics and other manufacturers to keep their knowledge current with changes in technology. Team members use detectors from KELLYCO stock, not special units provided by any factory. These stock detectors are then used in daily coin and treasure hunting under the same conditions any detector owner would expect to face and the testing is done over all different types of soils. The results of this testing helps bring about industry and product changes and improvements. "Consumer reports" by KELLYCO help all persons interested in this fascinating hobby to acquire greater knowledge so that he or she may be assured that the detector they purchase is electronically advanced, and most importantly, tested and certified to be THE BEST AVAILABLE FOR THE PRICE!

Ram Publications

Complete VLF-TR Metal Detector Handbook (The)
Thoroughly explains VLF/TR metal/mineral detectors and
HOW TO USE them. Compares VLF/TR's with all other types.

Detector Owner's Field Manual
Explains total capabilities and HOW TO USE procedures of all types of
metal detectors.

Electronic Prospecting
Learn how to find gold and silver veins, pockets, and nuggets using easy
electronic metal detector methods.

Gold Panning Is Easy
This excellent field guide shows you how to FIND and PAN gold as quickly
and easily as a professional.

Modern Metal Detectors
This advanced handbook for home, field, and classroom study gives the
expertise you need for success in any metal detecting situation, hobby or
professional, and increases your understanding of all fields of metal detector use.

Professional Treasure Hunter
Discover how to succeed with PROFESSIONAL METHODS, PERSISTENCE,
and HARD WORK.

Robert Marx: Quest for Treasure
The exciting, almost unbelievable true account of the discovery and salvage
of the Spanish treasure galleon, *Nuestra Señora de la Maravilla,* lost at sea,
January 1656.

Successful Coin Hunting
The world's most authoritative guide to FINDING VALUABLE COINS with
all types of metal detectors. The name speaks for itself!

Treasure Hunter's Manual #6
Quickly guides the inexperienced beginner through the mysteries of FULL
TIME TREASURE HUNTING.

Treasure Hunter's Manual #7
The classic! THE book on professional methods of RESEARCH, RECOVERY,
and DISPOSITION of treasures found.

Treasure Hunting Pays Off!
An excellent introduction to all facets of treasure hunting.

Weekend Prospecting!
Written for the person who wants to know exactly how to get started in the
fascinating and rewarding hobby of weekend prospecting with metal detectors
and gold panning equipment.

ON THE COVER...

COINS FROM CHARLES GARRETT'S PERSONAL COLLECTION

Any coin hunter through proper searching can add to his collection many of the well-known Buffalo nickels, reminders of our country's adventurous years. The Liberty Walking half-dollar, a prize in any coin collection, can still be discovered in abundance. The Army and Navy Civil War token brings nostalgic recollections of the colorful beginning of a truly United States and its progress into the Industrial Revolution. The greatly sought-after American gold coins minted from gold produced by the toil of the American prospector can, with persistent effort, be added to the coin hunter's collection. Typical of the rarer coins which greatly enhance any coin collection is the 1802, 2 over 1, Draped Bust silver dollar. With proper knowledge of where to look and the most effective ways to search, your reward can be the recovery of valuable coins such as these... and thousands more like them.

By CHARLES GARRETT
Modern Metal Detectors
Successful Coin Hunting
Treasure Hunting Pays Off!
Treasure Hunting Secrets
Electronic Prospecting (with Lagal)
Complete VLF-TR Metal Detector Handbook (The) (with Lagal)

SUCCESSFUL
Coin Hunting

by

CHARLES GARRETT

RAM BOOKS

ISBN 0-915920-47-6
Library of Congress Catalog Card No. 73-87120
Successful Coin Hunting
© Copyright 1974. © Copyright rev. 1976 ed. © Copyright rev. 1978 ed.
© Copyright 1979. © Copyright 1981. © Copyright 1982.
© Copyright rev. 1984 ed. © Copyright rev. 1985 ed.
Charles L. Garrett.

First printing November 1974 • Eighteenth printing June 1987

With each printing, *Successful Coin Hunting* is revised as necessary to
keep the text current.

Cover Design: Ron Speed

For FREE listing of related treasure hunting books write
Ram Publishing Company • P.O. 38649 • Dallas, Texas 75238

This book is dedicated to our special son, Charles Lewis, who incurred brain damage at an early age. Above our sorrow, we believe that perhaps God permits mental retardation in order to give mankind a glimpse of the perfect, God-created man ... one without envy and hate within his thoughts ... one wherein only the purest kind of love is possible.

Charles and Eleanor Garrett

If you will seek God's wisdom with the same zeal and effort that you seek money and hidden treasures, you will find happiness, long life, riches, honor, and peace.

Proverbs 2:4-5; 3:13, 16-17 (paraphrased)

CONTENTS

FOREWORD

When I was invited to write the introduction to SUC-CESSFUL COIN HUNTING — I at first refused! I thought, "There are dozens of highly qualified writers who could do a much better job." However, Charles insisted, saying he knew my words would be honest and straightforward. He didn't realize he thus provided me with words which describe him to a "T". This is no testamonial or praise afforded to one's best friend; it is to give credit where credit is due.

Charles Garrett is beyond doubt the most respected authority on advanced metal detecting equipment in the field today. He was voted Manufacturer of the Year in 1973 at the annual treasure hunters' convention held at Oklahoma City's Shepherd Mall under the direction of Bob Barnes. Since this award is voted upon by other top manufacturers and recognized treasure hunters, there could be no greater honor. Because most manufacturers are engineering experts, devoting most of their time to design and production, it is indeed a rarity to see an electronic specialist who is also one of today's most successful coin hunters and all-around treasure seekers. Charles has left his mark on the metal detector industry with his numerous inventions, including his patented "Zero Drift" circuitry.

SUCCESSFUL COIN HUNTING is a book that will astonish you and challenge your imagination. It will help both the beginner or professional gain knowledge on "where" and "how". Charles has gone beyond other writers in the field of coin hunting in the amount and quality of specific information he has set down. In addition to his own knowledge, he also shares many, many tips, ideas and pictures from a number of other experienced and professional coin seekers from all parts of the country. The book is filled with excellent photographs showing actual finds and individual coin hunting methods. By combining his extensive knowledge of electronic equipment with his long experience in the fascinating hobby of coin hunting, Charles has been able to produce a masterpiece of instructive literature — a classic book in the field that may never be surpassed.

If I sound biased and impressed by SUCCESSFUL COIN HUNTING, I intend to! When you have read your copy, you will understand why. You will recommend it enthusiastically to your friends as the most complete and instructive coin hunting manual you have ever read.

I thank Charles for the opportunity to write this introduction. I am proud to be a part of his book and to count myself among the millions who have the honor of knowing this unselfish and humble man, my friend, Charles Garrett.

Roy Lagal
Lewiston, Idaho

WHY DID I WRITE SUCCESSFUL COIN HUNTING?

I wrote this book because I want to pass on to you, the coin hunter, the things I have learned about coin hunting. I believe the beginning coin hunter should learn as much as possible about the hobby before starting out. Hopefully, the book will give you a head start down the road of successful coin hunting.

Perhaps the information included herein will not be of much value to the seasoned coin hunter. Many coin hunters are more active and experienced than I. Nevertheless some of the tips and techniques contained in the following pages may be of value to these persons. The discussions on the different detector types, their operation and applications, may benefit even the "old salt". Several basic types of coin hunting detectors are on the market, including the BFO, the TR, the VLF and the new VLF/TR's, and others ... but, to my knowledge, there is no complete guideline written which explains all the different instruments, their peculiarities and operating characteristics, and how they are best suited for the many different coin hunting applications.

So, my purpose is this: to help all *new* coin hunters become *successful* coin hunters. To them I offer my twenty-plus years of "how to", "where to", and "when to" coin hunting knowledge. To the already experienced and successful coin hunters I offer possibly a few new coin hunting tips, but, more fittingly, my total sympathy for those breaking backs that remind us all of the successful coin hunting days we have had. To all detector operators, I offer the detector knowledge related to coin hunting that I have gained from the building, testing and use of detectors in coin hunting.

Throughout the book are tips and suggestions that have been submitted by many coin hunters. Credit has been given when at all possible. Many of the pictures were contributed by successful coin hunters. Their names are given in the picture captions.

Charles Garrett

This photograph of the author, taken in Australia, is included in SUCCESSFUL COIN HUNTING as an example of how treasure hunting has become international in scope and how people the world over are interested in successful treasure stories. Charles is holding a 22 troy ounce gold nugget that was found in Western Australia's desert outback region. The nugget is just one of countless quantities of nuggets that are being found the world over by users of the new VLF/TR deep seeking detectors. The discovery of the nugget pictured here was given world-wide publicity. There is no doubt that treasure hunting has now become an internationally recognized hobby, one in which families and people of all ages can take part, not just a sport undertaken by a few adventurous individuals.

CHAPTER 1

To Begin With...

Coin hunting is the searching for and retrieving of lost coins. Countless millions of coins have been lost and await recovery by the metal detector hobbyist. Thousands of Indianhead and Wheat pennies, Buffalo nickels, Barber dimes, Liberty and Washington quarters, Liberty Walking half-dollars, and many other types of coins are being recovered every day. And, it appears people are losing more coins today than the coin hunter is finding. Coins are lost everywhere people go; coins are being found everywhere people have been. These facts support the reasons why this aspect of treasure hunting is believed to be the fastest growing hobby in America.

FIVE THOUSAND COINS CAN BE YOURS

The person not familiar with the hobby of coin hunting finds it difficult to believe that coins can be found. "Who loses coins?", they say. "Surely there are not enough lost coins to make it worth while to buy a metal detector to go out and spend time looking for them!" A fitting reply is . . . any active and experienced coin hunter can find five thousand coins each year. This is only an average of 100 coins found each weekend for fifty weeks . . . a reasonable and obtainable goal. On any given weekend an experienced coin hunter can find from 100 to 500 coins. However, this same person would not find any coins in this same length of time if he did not follow the rules he has learned in coin hunting. A coin hunter *must* search for coins where they are lost, and they are lost where people have been. It is easy after a short time to learn the best places to search for coins, and there are hundreds of "best places".

"ZIP, ZIP, ZIP, ZIP, ZIP!"

At the site of an old drive-in theater my father and I found more than 250 coins in an area eighteen feet square. We recovered these coins from the small area immediately in front of the projection booth in a period of less than ninety minutes. Around the perimeter of this area a pipe railing had been built to keep persons from walking in front of the projector lights. Apparently this railing drew kids like a magnet. They must have used it to climb on, swing on, tumble on, "ride horses" on, and for all other sorts of gymnastics. The majority of the coins were found beneath

1

Wayne Garrett, the author's father, digs a coin in front of a drive-in theater projection booth. It was in this small area that the author and his father found more than 250 coins.

this fence and on both sides to approximately two feet out. Sometimes the coins came out in bunches in clumps of dirt. When I made the first sweep, the detector speaker went, "zip, zip, zip, zip, zip!" I thought, "There are surely lots of pulltabs here." All of these "zips" were, however, money "zips"!

BENEFITS AND SUCCESS CAN BE OBTAINED

This is just a typical example of the success which can be obtained by the coin hunter. Many coins commonly found in old areas are worth from several times their face value, up to several dollars. Often the numismatic value of an occasional coin which the coin hunter retrieves can pay for a detector with some left over! Occasionally, coins recovered are worth up to many thousands of dollars. And don't forget the "value" in rediscovering a moment of the past. Each time a coin is lost a moment of life is preserved until someone finds that coin.

2

All of these old and valuable coins and jewelry items were found by L. L. "Abe" Lincoln during his many explorations into the old gold mining camps of Idaho.

Ask any coin hunter what he thinks about coin hunting. You will find unanimous support in favor of this rewarding hobby. Health benefits come right along with the monetary returns and the fun of getting out into the fresh air and sunshine. In fact, the main reason I search for treasure and hunt coins is that I am primarily interested in the health benefits I receive. When I find coins and other valuables, I consider this the added benefit of treasure hunting . . . the frosting on the cake!

Just how successful each coin hunter is depends upon, for one thing, how carefully he selected his detecting instrument and how well he has mastered its use. There are over 250 different brands and models of instruments from which to choose. Most of these can be grouped into only a handful of categories. Each category deserves individual attention and discussion. All persons really serious about coin hunting should study these discussions, especially those related to the type of instrument he or she prefers. There are many "tricks" and techniques which the detector operator must know in order to receive maximum benefits and results from using a detection instrument.

3

Well, let's get started. I'm happy you are coming along with me. We will venture from the coast to the mountains, from the snow to the desert. Coin hunting is fun and rewarding. You'll see!

It was here that the author wrote portions of SUCCESSFUL COIN HUNTING. This view from the author's van is part of Audubon Park in Garland, Texas. Portions of the book were also written in the Big Bend National Park of West Texas.

CHAPTER II

Who Coin Hunts?

As you search for coins you will encounter coin hunting youngsters from ages four to beyond age eighty. There is no age limit. Coin hunting is popular because it is fun and rewarding. Even though detectors have been around for many years, coin hunting has carved a notch for itself in the outdoor hobby world just during the last few years. Coin hunting, like treasure hunting, is becoming more and more a family hobby. Wives are becoming as avid coin and treasure hunters as husbands; and the children are beginning to join in! I have seen some young children who could find more coins than could their parents. Many people coin hunt for the fun of it, as well as for the relaxation and good exercise they get. It gives people something interesting to do. It not only is relaxing mentally and physically, but is also rewarding in many other ways. More and more camp-

This little girl tries her hand at coin finding during a THAP competition meet in Houston. Many young children are avid coin hunters. Some of them find more coins than their parents!

These two ladies proudly display the trophies and instruments they won at a competition meet at California City, California. The meet was sponsored by the Prospector's Club of Southern California (PCSC).

ers, hunters, fishermen, vacationers and back-packers are adding coin hunting instruments to their sports gear. They are finding that coin hunting is filling gaps in their regular sports and other outdoor activities, and provides added enjoyment for all members of the family.

COIN HUNTING IS PROFITABLE

Since searching for lost coins is profitable, as well as relatively simple and easy, coin hunting has become the most popular hobby in the world of treasure hunting. People who have no interest at all in seeking large treasures enjoy coin hunting. Many persons, however, who begin with coin hunting gradually extend their new hobby into the other areas of treasure hunting. Coin Hunting, Relic Hunting, Ghostowning, Bottle Hunting, Prospecting, Nugget Hunting, and, of course, General Treasure and Cache Hunting are all engaged in by metal detector operators. Actually, the "old pro" treasure hunter of yesterday is fading, being replaced rapidly by the everyday hobbyist. It is perhaps one of the most fascinating and interesting pastimes ever to capture the imagination of the world.

6

Lucile Bowen, Spokane, Washington, displays a few of her more valued finds. Note that the bottle in the center of the picture is covered with coins, jewelry, and other artifacts which have been found. Lucile states that Clarence Bullard, retired fire department captain, was perhaps the first person ever to display his finds on bottles in this way. Mr. and Mrs. Harry Bowen are active members of the Northwest Treasure Hunters Club of Spokane.

IT IS HEALTHFUL

Many people begin to coin hunt because it is an easy and perfect way to achieve physical fitness. One of the most valuable fringe benefits of the metal detecting hobby is the health benefit. Along with the purchase and regular use of a metal detector comes a built-in body building program. Leg muscles firm up; the flab around the middle begins to diminish as excess pounds drop off. Breathing improves, and the old "ticker" ticks more steadily. At night people who have coin hunted all day sleep like the proverbial log! Coin hunting can be excellent therapy for many who are recovering from an operation or an illness. This hobby will take such people out-of-doors into the fresh air and sunshine. There are many who have rapidly recuperated from long illnesses and operations when they earnestly began the hobby of coin hunting. Even people with heart problems, who need exercise but cannot overdo, find coin hunting a wonderful method to obtain just the exercise they need.

10% DON'T HUNT COINS

It is surprising but true that at least 90% of all detector owners coin hunt at one time or another. Approximately 60% of all owners use their detectors primarily for coin

These four people from Farmington, New Mexico, have been searching for coins for a long time. They have found approximately 45,000 coins during their many hunting expeditions. Left to right: Ray and Frankie Willerford, Dolly and Don Lewis.

hunting and only occasionally get involved in other forms of treasure hunting. About 20% of these people become quite adept at coin hunting, and could be called professionals. They spend most of their free time coin hunting and looking for places to coin hunt. Approximately 30% of all coin hunters are women, and the percentage is increasing. My estimates come from the letters I receive, people I talk with, and from the general sources of information about treasure hunting to which I am exposed.

TREASURE HUNTERS ARE FINE PEOPLE

There are no finer people than today's treasure hunters. I have come to know thousands of these wonderful people, and I am convinced they are among the best. They are hard-working people who enjoy nature and the out-of-doors, and who truly enjoy a good day's work and the rewards it brings. Treasure hunters are here to stay.

This family has just completed their first coin hunt. They found a small handful of coins at this old house. In a very short time, as they gain experience in their new hobby, they will have filled the jar and many more like it.

9

CHAPTER III

Coin Hunters Find Coins and Other Things

The quantity of coins found by experienced coin hunters is in direct proportion to the amount of time and effort they spend in their search for coins. Five thousand coins per year is an easily attainable quantity. A good coin hunter who is active will find many more than that. Even though the minimum face value of five thousand coins might be only $250.00, the numismatic value of some of the coins could cause the total value to skyrocket. And, don't forget, other than coins, additional items, such as rings, jewelry, tokens, medallions, and similarly valuable artifacts, will be found. The value of the gold and silver in jewelry will always remain high, and today there is a tremendous market for artifacts.

THE REAL THING

In this book you will find many pictures of coin collections and other valuables amassed solely from coin hunting. These pictures are not faked in order to induce people to start coin hunting. I simply want to present the facts as they are, and to instruct, to the best of my capability, persons interested in the art of coin hunting. I have in my files many more pictures of people proudly displaying their coin finds. There was just not space enough in the book for them all. Some of these collections are truly small fortunes. I am constantly amazed at the quantity of wealth which today's coin hunter and treasure hunter is retrieving from the ground.

WHAT ELSE DO THEY FIND?

In addition to coins the coin hunter finds rings, medallions, trade tokens, small metal toys, keys, tools (such as screwdrivers and pliers), caches of buried treasure, and innumerable other items of value. Lest you think I am leading you astray, the coin hunter also retrieves vast quantities of nails, bottle caps, pulltabs, wire, tinfoil, metal foil gum wrappers and cigarette packages, bits of metal, knives, ejected cartridges, automobile parts, hinges, locks, *etc.* The list is endless. When Harry and Lucile Bowen of Spokane, Washington, go coin hunting, they wear an apron similar to the standard carpenter's apron. These coin hunters' aprons have two pockets in the front . . . the pocket on the right is labeled "goodies"; the pocket on the left is labeled

Bob Griffin proudly displays a portion of the coins and jewelry he has discovered during the past few years. He is an extremely active and successful California coin hunter who has found a profitable and healthful hobby.

11

Peter Bridge, Hesperian Detectors, P. O. Box 317, Victoria Park 6100, Western Australia, and Charles Garrett talk treasure in the Garrett Electronics museum. Peter pioneered a move to introduce professional treasure hunting and prospecting to Australia. The lower photograph shows one of many gold nuggets which was found recently in Western Australia. The nugget weighs 22 troy ounces. It is valued at approximately $30,000. Mr. Bridge is Garrett's Australian detector distributor. Should your travels ever take you to his fine country, contact him. He can show you the way to the gold country!

12

Ghostowning for coins is becoming increasingly popular, but as you search ghost towns, as well as other deserted homestead sites, be prepared to find relics like this one.

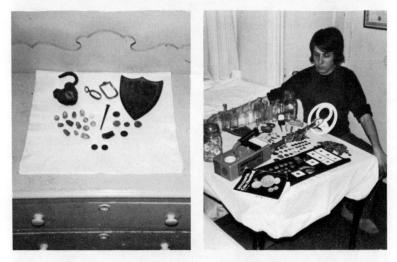

Thanks to Carl Young, Arlington, Virginia, for sending these good photos of some of his finds. He lives near a park which was once the site of a Civil War fort. He has found many relics and old coins at this location (photo on right). He specializes in searching old church sites, however, and on one short afternoon found twenty-two early date Lincoln pennies, an 1858 Flying Eagle cent, three Indianhead pennies (the oldest dated 1887), a 1910 Barber dime and a 1936 half-dollar. It all sounds great, Carl. Keep up the good work!

13

While her husband, Richard, was searching under the porch of an old movie lot false-front building, Nancy Waters searched around an old burned house. She found this .32 caliber pistol, the watch, the lighters, and other artifacts. Note the peculiarly-carved ring that Nancy is holding. It can also be seen in the picture inset in the upper right corner of this page. The outline of the face can barely be seen. The ring is lying at the end of the fork.

14

This coin hunter has surely amassed an unusual collection of guns, relics, watches, and coins found during the search of a long-abandoned, forgotten ghost town. His search was concentrated around the old stores, saloons, and other places where money changed hands.

"not so goodies". They place coins and other valuables in the "goodies" pocket and the junk items in the "not so goodies" pocket. Later on I'll tell you why they "keep" the junk or the non-valuables.

HIDDEN CACHES

Occasionally the coin hunter will find hidden caches such as a jar filled with coins and other valuables. Recently a coin hunter found 838 Buffalo nickels buried in an old quart-sized Mason jar. Quite often "hot" money is found . . . ill-gotten money which is secretly cached because nothing else can be done with it. Weapons like guns, knives, and swords are found. It seems that each outing turns up peculiar things. Recently I retrieved six, three-inch-diameter rusty steel washers from one hole. Apparently someone, when they finished pitching washers, left them in the hole and did not come back to recover them. Virgil Hutton found three silver dollars in another hole, all neatly stacked one on top of the other, at a city park in Austin, Texas.

15

This durable, rugged "goodies bag" is specially designed for the coin hunter. The extra-deep pockets prevent coins from falling out as the hunter bends and stoops while searching for coins. The waterproof Naugahyde plastic prevents moisture from the coins and loose dirt from soaking through to soil coin hunters' clothes. This particular type of bag is available from Garrett Electronics.

GOLD PIECE

Mr. Chet Blanchard recently made an unusual discovery; he found a two-and-a-half-dollar gold piece inside an old iron ten cent bank. During a treasure hunting show in Austin he left the exhibition building to try out a detector. He went searching around the parking meters on the street. He got an indication; dug up the object; saw it was a rusty piece of iron; and started to cast it aside. However, his eyes caught the glimmer of something shiny. He pried open the small iron container with a knife, and out fell the gold piece, valued at many times its face value. One of the thrills of coin hunting is that you never know what you'll dig up next!

GUN CACHE

Throughout this book you will find many photos showing things other than coins that have been found. I have described in this volume many things discovered by coin hunters. The coin hunter who is active quickly learns to expect the unreal. Recently a treasure hunter whom I must call "Bob" was searching an old ghost town ruins ten miles

Eight-hundred and thirty-eight Buffalo nickels were in this jar when it was found in the wall of an old building in East Texas.

A coin hunter's delight! Bill Mason, St. Paul, Minnesota, discovered these two small coin caches while searching old farm houses. A coin hunter often will discover such long-forgotten coin caches as the two shown above.

17

ROMAN

English Army officer Lt. Col. (Ret.) Jonathan Patterson found these Roman coins in Southern Europe. The coins date A. D. 190.

from Carthage, Texas. He was searching through a very old building walking along on the floor inside, scanning the floor in an attempt to locate coins that might have become lodged in the cracks in the boards. His detector gave an indication over an area as large as a tub. He carefully lifted several boards from the floor only to expose the ground a few inches below. On probing in the dirt he struck wood. After about an hour's work he uncovered a box filled with fifty ninety-year-old-plus rifles and several handguns. The box they were placed in was so deteriorated that it crumbled at a touch. All the weapons, however, had been carefully preserved with some kind of grease. The guns were mostly flintlocks and ball and cap rifles. Bob knew the owner of the building, and, on inquiry, the man told Bob he had owned the ghost town for ninety years and did not know anything about the guns. What a prize this turned out to be! I have seven of these old rifles in my museum at Garrett Electronics, 2814 National Drive, Garland, Texas. Displayed along with the guns are hundreds of other items that treasure hunters have found — guns, knives, swords, pistols, coins, jewelry, Civil War relics, farm implements and tools, Wells Fargo boxes and related items, Indian relics, and many similar treasures. Any time you are in the Dallas area do not fail to drive out to take a look and browse through this museum—it's free! It is always an enlightening experience to see other things that coin hunters and treasure hunters have found.

Many things are found by coin hunters. These things in this Garrett Electronics museum showcase are typical of the "other" items coin hunters find in ghost towns, around old buildings, etc.

CHAPTER IV

Where Do Coin Hunters Find Coins?

That's easy! Anywhere people have been—which is practically everywhere. Once a person has begun this hobby he will no longer need convincing that coins are to be found. He will soon have the problem of so many places to search he will have difficulty deciding where to go next. The number of places to search is all but endless! In the next chapter I have included a list of places where coins are found, with a brief description of where to look for coins in these places. The list is not all-inclusive, and could never be. New coin hunting locations are added to such a list daily. People write telling me about new discoveries. I pick up many valuable leads from newspapers, club bulletins, and other publications written about people. Oldtimers can tell you of places you could never learn about from other sources. Use your head; think. For instance, I searched for years before I suddenly realized that coin hunters should be able to find coins under the clothesline. And, sure enough, they were there. You can easily prove to yourself that mothers are unable to completely remove all coins and metal objects from the pockets of their little boys' and husbands' clothes before washing and hanging them to dry.

GOLD COINS PUT RIP VAN WINKLE TO SHAME

While on vacation with my family I struck up a conversation with a retired postman in a small north central Colorado town. He told me about a long-forgotten city park where an annual event had been held celebrating the founding of the city in the late 1800's. Since gold was plentiful in that gold mining town, the city fathers would go out the night before the day of the celebration and bury $5.00 gold pieces throughout the park. Beginning early the next morning, following a gunshot, anyone who wished could race out onto the field and begin scratching in the ground for these gold coins. Any detector operator could immediately see the value in searching this area. For seventy years gold coins have "slept" just beneath the surface, waiting for someone to come along with a metal detector. There are many such areas throughout the United States.

Here Dick Waters of San Fernando, California, crawls out from under a saloon/hotel building on the movie ranch studio lot. All of these coins and artifacts were found under the porch.

Here is where research paid off! These Caloosa Indian ornaments, plus many coins dating back to 1698 and several priceless relics, were found on an island off the coast of Florida. The large disk was used to hold their topknot or sprig of hair. The arrowhead is made of silver and is very rare. It was probably worn in a fashion similar to the other beads and silver ornaments shown in the photograph. The bead lying just below the arrowhead is gold and was probably made from a Spanish coin. To the right is a lead bead which is one of a kind. The other beads are Spanish trade beads. Many silver and gold Spanish coins have been found. The estimated value of the Indian "trinkets" shown in the photograph is $1,000.

21

"Beginner's luck"! Fred Mott, well-known treasure hunter, took his wife along on a coin hunting expedition and she found 426 coins, a ring, an antique bracelet, and the other old miscellaneous farm implements as shown. Mrs. Mott searched for two days around several old farm houses and other areas while Fred researched a treasure lead.

REWARDS BEGIN AT HOME

Above all, don't make the mistake of believing there are no coins to be found where you live. If you don't have the experience now, you soon will gain the knowledge to convince yourself that coins are truly found everywhere. The first place every person should start is right in his own backyard, branching out from there. The reason for writing this paragraph is that I have encountered many people who told me there was nothing in their areas worth searching for! The truth is, it would take an army of thousands of coin hunters, working many years, to search and clean out all the productive areas in the United States.

THE EAST COAST IS GOOD, REALLY!

I have had many Easterners tell me that metal detectors are useless along the East Coast because there is nothing there to be found. The first time I heard this I could not understand how anyone could believe it, until I began to think about it. Detectors had their beginning on the West Coast where they were utilized primarily for prospecting

Just think of the stories this old bench could tell! A coin hunter's heart would beat with excitement at the sight of this resting place where many coins and other valuables are surely buried in the ground.

and deep vein searching. Most of the instruments manufactured in the early years were manufactured on the West Coast. The majority of gold and other precious metals were found on the West Coast, with perhaps isolated exceptions like the state of Georgia. Consequently, people on the East Coast generally think of metal detectors as being of value only in the search for precious metals; they "logically" conclude that detectors are useless on the East Coast. Of course, this is very far from the truth. The East Coast is one of the hottest coin hunting areas. Since this section of the United States was settled first, more old and often more valuable coins and artifacts have been lost there.

In searching on the East Coast, or anywhere in the United States or the world, the same basic rules given in this book apply. You will search the same kinds of places, using the same detector operating techniques. The rewards are yours. Study your local history, talk to the old-timers, determine where the old parks, meeting grounds, old towns and communities were located. Here you will find the "hot spots". Here you will find the old and valuable coins that will make coin hunting really pay off.

The author searches for coins lost by youngsters as they climbed and played in this tree. There are always many "extra good" areas in parks and playgrounds. Take the time to find them.

STOP, LOOK . . .

In any given search area you will find there are "hot spots". In other words, persons are more apt to congregate in certain areas than in others. You can learn where these "hot spots" are by simply observing people. Drive over to your school or college campus, or when you are at church watch the people . . . see where they congregate, see where they stand and talk, see where the kids run and play. Go to schools and churches early to learn where cars unload their passengers. A little common sense and observation will greatly speed up your search and increase your take. In a children's park and playground area some of the better places to search are under swings, slides and tumble gyms. Naturally, children turning head over heels lose coins. Picnic areas and lovers' lanes are good because people usually sit or lie down. Coins are quite commonly lost in such areas. Drive-in theaters are excellent locations. In areas no longer used by the public you will have to use your own past experience or some self-learned criss-cross metal detection method in order to locate the "hot spots". As you search different areas, keep accurate count of the coins and jewelry you find and where you found them. From this data you will soon learn the probable location of the best places to search.

24

...AND LISTEN

Where were the old schools and academies located fifty or one hundred years ago? The training camps, CCC camps, campgrounds, settlers' encampments, parks, churches and missions? Where were old settlements in your area, the old ghost towns? In your home town where are the long-forgotten fairgrounds, circus and carnival areas? The old train station or the old swimming pools and picnic areas? You cannot possibly know of all the rewarding coin hunting areas in your town. Make it a habit to talk to family, friends, old-timers, storekeepers—particularly the older, retired people of the community who were postmen, bus drivers, merchants, policemen, firemen, and so on. These people will have a wealth of information to give you that will help you locate valuable coin hunting areas. Ask your parents or grandparents where the lovers' lanes of their day were. Check the city records. What about the parks? How old are they? Are they in the same place now they were fifty, seventy-five or one hundred years ago? What about downtown vacant lots? What used to be there? As you drive through rural communities, small towns and suburbs, stop to check with the old-time residents . . . and listen to them talk! Inquire where the general store, saloons, banks, and and cafes used to be.

This old CCC Camp of the '30's, located near Pennington, Texas, has probably never been searched. Surely it cointains many valuable coins.

25

EXAMPLES WILL HELP

A few examples will give you an idea of what I mean. Approximately one-half mile south from the town of Pennington, Texas, on the east side of the highway, is the site of the long-gone Steele Academy. This was a training school for boys which was in operation for many years, but its doors were closed well before the turn of the century. This should be a good coin hunting area.

From information gathered from the museum curator in the town of Cripple Creek, Colorado, I found the location of an old picnic grounds, high above the city on a mountain top. This park and picnic area was once so popular that the local trolley car company built a track all the way to the park and had cars running continuously, especially on weekends. There must be untold thousands of 75-100-year-old coins still awaiting the metal detecting coin hunter.

In Dallas, Texas, there is a park that has been in use since before the turn of the century. Many valuable coins have been recovered after their long interment.

THERE'LL BE A HOT TIME IN THE OLD TOWN!

One excellent method for finding the oldest coins is to locate geographically where your town or city was located when it was founded. Often the present town site is not located where the original townsite was. The "original" town of San Diego is a few miles north of the present downtown area. Recently my family and I visited "Old Town" San Diego and talked with George Mroczkowski. He showed us where he had excavated at the site of some old buildings. He uncovered many artifacts and valuable coins. These items are on display at 2493 San Diego Avenue.

The Bill Wendels of Florida learned the location of the original fort of Tampa, Florida. Many relics and coins including Spanish *reales*, half dimes, large cents, and other denominations have been found. The American coins are dated in the 1830's. Even older coins could still be found because the original town of Tampa was erected just outside Fort Brooke's walls in 1823.

LET'S FACE IT!

There is no doubt that most coin hunters truly enjoy getting out into the parks, playgrounds, and other areas to search for lost coins and valuables. But, let's face it — the greater the value of our finds, the more we enjoy and benefit financially from the hobby. Thus, it behooves us to make the most diligent efforts to seek out and locate the coin hunting areas where the most coins of most value are to be found. Granted, we all are thrilled when we dig up each

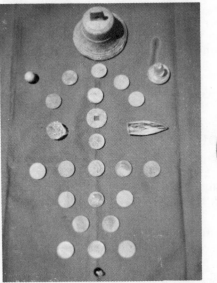

George Mroczkowski, president of the San Diego Gem and Treasure Hunting Association, and Kathryn Boone, along with several other club members, excavated a site located at Old Town, San Diego. They excavated to a depth of four feet and discovered many coins and valuable artifacts, a few of which are shown above. The single coin is a gold ducat which was minted in Venice between 1788 and 1797. The story of digging in Old Town and many others are found in George's new book, GEORGE MROCZKOWSKI, PROFESSIONAL TREASURE HUNTER, published by Ram Publishing Company. George tells of found gold coins, Spanish treasure, and multi-million dollar treasure searches in this hard to put down treasure book.

coin, even though it may be of modern-day vintage and worth only face value. However, there is within all of us the desire to locate the half cents, the large cents, the two and three cent pieces, the half dimes, and Liberty-seated quarters, and many other older coins ... the coins worth many times, maybe even thousands of times, their face value. These extra-value coins are generally not located in parks, around school yards, or in areas of relatively recent construction. You must look for older construction and areas of activity to find the rarer coins. There is where research pays off!

NEWSPAPERS

Make it a daily habit to read the lost-and-found section. Quite often persons losing valuables will advertise and post a reward for the return of these objects. You can contact these people and make prior agreements with them as to the value of your remuneration or reward should you be successful in locating their lost property. Newspapers are filled with information on locations of public congregations (company picnics, family reunions, and so on). Spend time at the library or your newspaper office reviewing yesteryear's newspapers. You will find the location of old parks and playgrounds, band concert sites, fairground and circus lots, and information on public activities that occurred in the past, as well as notices of lost articles. Only your efforts will limit you here, and ... if you are a treasure hunter, you will find many heart-fluttering treasure location possibilities.

"AT YOUR SERVICE"

Bulletin boards in laundromats and drug stores and other public areas many times have notices of lost items. It will pay to check these places frequently. Why not post your own "Have detector, will travel" notices on these free bulletin boards!

It is a good idea to make contact with the police and your insurance agent, or even all of the agents in your home town. Tell them you have a detector, and that you are willing to help them locate lost jewelry and other valuables. You may be surprised at the services you can perform, as well as the monetary rewards you will receive. There is no reason why the owner of a metal detector cannot greatly increase his annual income with just a reasonable amount of thought and physical effort. In times of an economic depression, the well-trained detector operator can have more money than he will know what to do with.

IT'S UP TO YOU

I cannot stress too strongly that you must give thought to these things! The true monetary value in coin hunting and the greatest personal rewards come from finding the old, valuable coins as a result of your own research, investigation, and hard work. While you may grow tired of digging up recent issue coins in parks and playgrounds, even if you come home with your pockets full each time, you *won't* grow tired of digging up old and rare coins in places you have found by your own desire and careful investigative efforts. You will only become even more enthusiastic, and your rewards will increase.

I have tried in this chapter to stir your imagination, to help you come to believe that coins are found everywhere. However, to greatly enhance the value and quantity of your take, I hope you understand that research and thought, planning and a lot of investigative work are necessary if you are to receive the maximum benefits of coin hunting. The next chapter will include as many places as I can think of or have learned about where coins have been and can be found. I have included a list of people you should listen to. Also, throughout the book you will find tidbits of information that will help you to research and locate additional places. As I stated earlier, your success depends entirely upon you. The coins are there. YOU can find them!

CHAPTER V

Places to Search... People to Listen to

PLACES

WHERE PEOPLE HAVE LIVED
Inside
Closets and shelves—single coins could lie unnoticed on old shelving

In the walls

Above and beneath door and window sills, in the doors (A $50 gold coin worth several thousand dollars was recently found between an old house window and the window sill.)

Underneath or along baseboards and quarter-rounds

Underneath and along edges of linoleum or other flooring, particularly beneath linoleum near holes in the linoleum

Old garages

Basements, sheds, barns, haylofts and other outbuildings, such as chicken houses, and other animal shelters

Crawl spaces under houses and other buildings

Outside
Your own backyard

Driveways . . . where persons would have gotten in or out of cars or wagons

Front doors . . . people reaching into pockets for keys might have dropped coins

Under houses, porches, and steps, especially those with handrails where children might have played and rolled coins through

Around and along all walks and paths

Around old outhouses—on the ground where the outhouses used to stand and the trails that led there from the main house

Around hitching posts and hitching post racks

Between gate posts

Around mail boxes, both rural and urban

Well and pump sites

Storm cellar and basement steps

Around old watering troughs

Along fence rows and around stiles

Under trees where children could have played or had swings and houses or where shade tree-mechanics might have worked. I remember as a child playing and swinging on many of the neighborhood trees. I am sure coins are still there.

Under clotheslines or in places they once stood, as well as along fences in rural areas where in years past clothes might have been hung to dry

Around patios and garden furniture areas . . . try those around old homes which might have permanently installed benches or rest areas

Areas where children may have had lemonade stands

WHERE PEOPLE HAVE BEEN

Recreation, amusement and camping areas

Fishing piers, boat ramps and landings

Ferryboat loading and unloading sites

Back-country fishing camps and health resorts

Abandoned resort areas of any kind

Horse and hiking trails where backpackers have made a habit of stopping, camping and spending the night

Swimming areas, especially old ones

Children's camps (during the off season) . . . concession areas, around cabin or tent sites, and areas where exercises might be performed or games played

Around ski tows and along the slopes

Beach swimming areas, particularly at low tide, and out into the water as deeply as you can submerge your search coil

Miniature golf courses and golf practice ranges

Shooting and target practice ranges—lots of shell casings, but coins as well

Any old springs where wagon trains or settlers might have stopped for the night. Incidentally old springs make excellent wishing wells and should be thoroughly cleaned

River fords

Bluffs and embankments where children might have slid on cardboard or snow sleds

Trailer park areas that have been struck by tornadoes and other severe storms . . . trailers may have been overturned and lost coins and valuables may not have been recovered.

Under stadium seats

Bandstands, gazebos, and other entertainment platforms . . . or where they might have been

Amusement parks and fairgrounds, carnival and circus sites . . . particularly where coin pitches and baseball throw booths may have stood (rings and watches could have been thrown off), around concession stand locations and ticket booths

Rodeo grounds and sites of early-day back lot horse races, towsack races, *etc.*

Race tracks and ramps for horses, cars or motorcycles

Parks—around benches; drinking fountains; under trees; around steps; under swings, slides, and tumble gyms; around little hills and valleys which might have attracted children; around and under picnic tables; baseball and football playing areas; lovers' lanes

Drive-in theaters . . . up front where generally children's playground equipment is provided, around speaker poles, concession stand areas, around the protected area in front of the projection booth, around ticket windows

Motels and trailer parks, around recreational areas like swimming pools, ice and concession machines

Around historical markers and highway state markers or any areas that are popular photographic spots

Tourist stops of any kind. For example, wishing wells and wishing bridges, hilltops overlooking large expanses of territory, mountain passes, scenic lookouts such as along the Blue Ridge Parkway and the Grand Canyon, below any kind of such look-outs or bridges and towers where people might have tossed coins for "luck"

Along highways, especially near litter cans. When throwing trash from cars, people occasionally lose rings, bracelets and other valuables. Children also are known to throw valuable things out of cars!

Footpaths and resting spots along the highways, roadside parks

OTHER IDEAS

Anywhere people congregate and anywhere people have been

Around service stations, particularly the older ones

In church yards where members might have stood to visit before and after the service; around trees where children played; around any steps, walks, and in passenger unloading areas; where tables were built to take care of meals or where there were "people all around, dinner on the ground" gatherings

Revival meeting sites, such as brush arbors

Cemeteries

Schools and colleges—around playground equipment, bicycle racks, just outside cafeteria doors where children might have lined up for lunch, drinking wells or fountains, shaded walk or rest areas. Go to these places to see where the students congregate.

Highway cafes and truck stops

Roadside stands, such as where fruits or vegetables might be (have been) sold

Around private clubs

Beaches near the site of suspected sunken ships, after the crowds have left, after rain storms or hurricanes. Around beach furniture

At the site of any fire, around burned buildings and houses. Here it is quite common to find clumps of coins that were melted together from the heat.

Disaster areas . . . Cripple Creek, Colorado fire; San Francisco earthquake; Austin, Pennsylvania flood, for example

At the site of train, auto or airplane wrecks

Lots where an old building has recently been torn down . . . lots of metal fragments but coins are there, too!

Areas where bulldozers have worked, particularly in an area where it has been reported that a bulldozer has uncovered money caches

Underneath any boardwalks

Ghost towns . . . along the boardwalks, in the streets

Around ladder or slide fire escapes permanently attached to buildings. As a kid I recall going over daily to the two-story church building and playing on the metal slide that provided the second-story church members a means of getting out in the event of fire.

Anywhere that cars park. Around parking meters and along the grassy strips where a car might be parked. Parking lots—especially along fences and where paper money could have been blown from the parking lots. Car wash and vacuum areas. Large department store or shopping center parking lots.

Stage stops and relay stations, trading posts

Old shipping pen areas and railroad depots

Trolley and bus stops. Don't pass up bus stops and pick up areas for school children.

Fronts of drive-in grocery shops

Telephone booths

Old bars, taverns, inns. Don't forget the local beer garden; the ones with a few inches of loose gravel can be rewarding.

33

Construction sites and businesses where catering trucks stop to sell food to employees

Fireplugs (dogs don't lose coins, but kids do when they play "jump the fireplug")

Nursing home lawns and walks, around seating areas

Fields and lots where fleamarkets and auctions are held

Courthouse lawns, around benches and walkways

Caves . . . *Caution:* Caves may produce more "bats than bucks"!

PEOPLE TO LISTEN TO

Contact your town's *police departments* and *personal property insurance agents* for the location of lost valuables

Highway clean-up crews for good locations. They may perhaps know of areas where they have found numerous coins and other valuables.

Lifeguard on duty at swimming areas. He might be able to tell you specific areas where people have lost their valuable jewelry.

Jewelry store clerks. They may know of women who have lost wedding and engagement rings. Since these lost rings must be replaced, the lady will go to the store to buy new rings. Perhaps while there she may tell the clerk her sad tale.

For the same reason, talk to the *clerk at the "dime store" jewelry counter.* Many couples who lose valuable engagement and wedding rings cannot afford immediately to replace them. During the time they are saving for new rings or waiting for newly-purchased rings to be correctly sized, they often purchase cheap rings for the wife to wear. Chances are quite good the wife will tell the clerk of her misfortune. Always, if possible, return valuable finds to the owner.

Whenever possible, talk to the *old-timers* and the *retired people* in any community. Most of them have a tremendous storehouse of possible locations.

Your *city firemen.* They can perhaps give you the locations of many old burned houses and stores which have never been rebuilt, but where the ground surely will contain many coins and relics.

Your minister. He may be able to guide you to many old and long-forgotten church yards and revival meeting places.

Historians and archaeologists. They may be able to give you the location of many old once-populated but long-deserted community sites.

34

Railroad engineers and conductors. They might know of the location of many old and forgotten railroad depots and other locations along the railroad right-of-way that are no longer in use but were once populated.

Bus drivers . . . Ask them where old, no longer used bus stops are located

Park and recreation area caretakers. They can tell you where people tend to congregate and the possible location of former bandstands, slides, swings, other playground equipment, and picnic tables.

Don't "talk to" but "listen to" *history books* written about your area. Read all the books you can on your local history. In all probability you will lay each book down and walk away armed with the knowledge of dozens of places that will yield large quantities of old and valuable coins. Most people think that research is dull, but that is far from the truth. Research is profitable in many different ways, and to me it is as much fun as the actual treasure hunt. Many people say, "Oh, I don't have time to research," but this is the wrong attitude. Actually the right kind of research helps you save time and greatly increase the value of your take. Spend time at your library or newspaper offices reviewing newspapers of yesteryear. You may not have time to search out all the possibilities you uncover! Visit museums and study maps for locations of old sites. Watch newspaper "lost and found" sections for possibilities.

Mr. & Mrs. Wayne Cummings, Davenport, Iowa, found all of these coins and valuables in the shallow water of a swimming hole near Shreveport, Louisiana.

These children play on a stairway on the main street of Cripple Creek, Colorado. Open stair steps and railings create "instant money" for the coin hunter.

All you need do to locate good coin areas is watch where children play.

36

CHAPTER VI

Town and City Coin Hunting

As you might expect, the majority of all coin hunting takes place in the cities, towns, and suburbs. It is in these places that people congregate. A complete list of places to coin hunt in communities would be unending. In this chapter I will discuss the more-frequently searched areas, and give a few ideas and hints that might help you in your coin hunting.

HOUSES AND HOMESTEADS

The most likely places to find coins around old homes are: around front porches and walks; in driveways where persons got in and out of cars, buggies, and wagons; around hitching posts; around back door steps; along any walk areas; under clotheslines; under and around trees where children may have played, had treehouses, or swung from ropes or swings suspended from tree limbs. Carefully search all old garages. Many coins are found in various places inside old houses. Such places include closet shelves where a single coin would lie unnoticed; between the walls, especially where a small child could push coins through tiny cracks; under rugs and carpets; in cracks in the floor; between the floor and the baseboards or quarter-rounds.

If any of the flooring in the house is linoleum tile carefully scan over this tile, particularly where there may be cracks in it. I have seen several individual coins found beneath tile such as this. Apparently the coins were placed there by young children. In addition to children pushing and hiding coins under holes and edges of linoleum, coins could also have been swept into these places by the lady of the house. A. T. Evans of Eureka Press and "Father" of the TREASURE HUNTERS YEARBOOKS, indicated that some very nice individual coins have been found between the baseboards and the floor, apparently swept underneath as the room was cleaned. Or, try under the doorsills where coins may also have been swept or pushed.

CHILDREN

Try to think as they might. Remember, you were once a child also! Where did you hide coins? As you search old houses look around the rooms and try to think like a child would. Even squat down so you place your head on the level of a child's. Look around the room and observe places coins

37

Charles Garrett searches the ruins of the 100-year-old South American city for coins, relics, and caches. There are so many good areas in the world to search that the author believes the treasure hunter will never be able to search them all. A treasure film, "Treasures of Mexico" was photographed here. Contact Customer Service Department, Garrett Electronics, 2814 National Drive, Garland, Texas 75041, 214-278-6151, if you wish a free loan of this twenty-minute 16 mm. color film to show to your club or group.

This is a portion of a recovered silver cache. All of these pieces were originally poured into crude molds. Most of them, as you can see, were then sized by cutting, thus producing "homemade" cobs or trading pieces. Age estimated to be 75 to 100 years.

could be stashed. Many reports have come in that coins have been found in door locks. Any type of lock with a keyhole large enough for a dime or penny to fit through is a good place to search, even though you might have to dismantle the lock. Just be sure, if you do this, that you place it back like it was.

THEY WERE IN THE DOOR

I received a telephone call the other day from a friend who spent an hour searching an old house and uncovered mostly junk and only a few coins. He had left his instrument on, and as he started to leave the house the search coil brushed against the wooden door. The instrument gave a loud squeal. He called it luck, but he found a whole cache of coins that apparently had been dropped, one at a time, down into this hollow door through a small slot found cut in the door.

WHO LEFT THE HALVES? SHE DID?

I remember an incident (call it "luck" also) when a carpenter was engaged to replace several rotting boards on the outside of an old house. As he began pulling off the rotten boards, half-dollars began pouring out of the wall onto the ground. Several hundred old Liberty Walking half-dollars were recovered. It was not certain as to how the coins came to be there; however, it is known that thirty years earlier the building had been a house of ill repute.

FUSE BOXES

While searching around old houses always look for the early style electrical fuse boxes. (Remember when people used pennies as fuses?) I can recall my grandmother placing pennies in the fuse boxes, instead of fuses, when she ironed. Apparently the iron drew more current than the fuse capability, and she had to beef up the current supply by letting the penny serve as the fuse. When you find these fuse boxes, look into the box to make sure there are no dirt-covered coins. *Caution:* always make certain the fuse boxes are disconnected from the power supply before attempting a hand search.

GOOD LUCK COINS

For some reason, people make it a habit to place "good luck" coins around the foundation piers of houses and other buildings. It is a superstition that you could capitalize on. Search around the corners of old houses, especially around sites where the houses have been torn down. A. T. Evans points out that in abandoned towns ruins of old courthouses can still be found. He says, "Find the cornerstone, and you are likely to reap a real treasure in both money and historical items. Remember the custom of placing various items and paraphenalia inside cornerstones goes far back, even prior to the turn of the century. It's a good idea if you make such a find to share the historical items with local museums or historical societies."

THEY DROPPED 'EM THROUGH THE FLOOR

Another good tip from A. T. Evans—"In Big Spring, Texas, a coin hunter chanced to overhear an elderly gentleman tell how, when a small boy, he and some friends used to snitch coins out of his father's cash drawer while he was busy barbering and drop them through cracks in the floor. Investigation by the coin hunter showed the old house to be still in the same location and, wonder of wonders, it was built on stilts so that the floor was some three feet above the ground, leaving plenty of room to crawl underneath with a detector. More than two-hundred old coins were found under this house."

OUTHOUSES

Don't laugh! These seem to be places to find coins, especially if the coin hunter can search the ground on which the old buildings stood. Apparently many coins fell from men's and boys' trousers, went through the cracks in the floor, and were gradually covered by fine dust and dirt. Search the trail that leads from the outhouse to the main house. Sometimes people were in quite a hurry to get out to this place to read the latest Montgomery Ward catalog. If you are interested in bottle hunting and in relic hunting, consider digging old outhouse pits. I realize this may sound quite repulsive; however many bottle diggers have assured me that after only a few years body wastes decompose and are in no way harmful . . . you might ask your doctor! This is one of the favorite digging places of bottle hunters, and small fortunes have been taken from these pits in the form of bottles, guns, coins, and other relics because when a pit was abandoned it was often used as a dump for discarded items.

PLAYGROUNDS AND PARKS

Playgrounds are high on the list of locations where coins are found in large quantity. It will pay you to make a trip to local playground areas and observe the children while they play. Always search carefully around all playground equipment. Rarely will a coin hunter fail to find a few coins around the see-saws, swings, tumble bars, and other climbing apparatus. Almost the entire playground area could be quite fruitfully searched. If there is a swimming pool be

Bob Bradshaw of Hurst, Texas, displays many of his finds. He searches primarily around old parks, circus and carnival lots, and downtown areas.

certain to search the grassy areas around it. Parents enjoy sitting around pools watching their children swim. Search around all drinking fountains, picnic tables and benches. Watch where the children play. Search all play areas — because there you will find coins.

Make an attempt to locate early maps of parks and playgrounds. I recall seeing a very old map of New York's Central Park. The *Smithsonian Magazine* printed this map along with a modern map in order to show the park's development. The old map showed the location of bandstands, concession stands, and other crowd-gathering locations no longer in existence. Such sites could prove very rewarding. George Sullivan, author of DO-IT-YOURSELF MOVING, says he knows a man who has recovered 30,000 coins from New York state parks. In the December 1968 issue of *National Geographic*, page 798, you will find a painstakingly prepared map of the old capital of the State of Virginia, Colonial Williamsburg. The artist has done a beautiful, three dimensional job of reconstructing on paper the old houses, churches, parks and playgrounds, schools, town buildings, and even an old Dutch-type windmill that probably drew crowds by the thousands, as they were located in 1780. The streets, alleys, and other area outlines are clearly shown. Anyone who wishes to use this map to guide him to good coin hunting areas at this site (if permission can be obtained) should be well rewarded.

LAKES

Quite often city lakes are dredged in order to deepen them and enhance the value of the lake. When this occurs in your city, try to locate the area where the dump dirt is taken. Scan this area for artifacts and other valuables. The bottoms of most lakes contain many lost and purposely discarded guns, fishing tackle, and other relics. By searching these dump sites perhaps you can recover some of the lost items.

These Spanish silver cobs, better known as "pieces of eight," were found on the beach near the site of an old sunken Spanish treasure ship. They were found by the Fantom Expeditions. Photo courtesy Ray Smith.

BLEACHERS AND STADIUM SEATS

Rarely will you ever fail to find coins under and around stadium seats. In addition to coins you will find watches, rings, knives, keys, and many other objects which have fallen through the stands. Spectators become quite excited at times and, without knowing it, they supply the treasure hunter with enough loot to fill his "goodies" pocket. Generally, these areas are cluttered with cans, bottles, cigarette packages, gum wrappers, and other bits of junk. Carry along a rake and perhaps a weed cutter to clean these areas for quicker searching. Also be on the lookout for paper money; occasionally you will find it.

FENCES ACCUMULATE MONEY

A thought just occurred to me which I have never passed on to anyone because I had forgotten about it. One day I drove over to a large shopping center. The parking lot around the center covers about ten acres. All along the north and west sides of this parking lot is a chain-link fence. The prevailing winds blow from the southeast to the northwest. Consequently, all paper and lightweight trash is blown along by the wind until it reaches the fence where it accumulates. That day, as I was leaving the lot, I spied a piece of paper money that was being blown along by the wind. Finally it came to rest among trash that had also blown into the fence. It was a $5.00 bill. There must be dozens of areas such as this in any town or city of moderate size. Here, of course, you don't need a metal detector. And, who knows what else you may find. It is just an idea I had to pass on; it might pay off for you.

CONCESSION STANDS AND TICKET BOOTHS

Concession stands and ticket booths were generally located in all areas where people congregated either to entertain themselves or to be entertained. Make a special effort to search both inside and outside of such stands. Also search out quite a way in front of the concession stands and ticket booths for the possible location of coins people dropped walking away from the stand with an armful of popped corn, peanuts, and hot dogs. In addition to coins, you may also find certain kinds of tokens, provided the ticket booths are old enough. Quite often patrons were issued tokens which could be redeemed at the same ticket windows at later events. It is not too uncommon to find such tokens, and they have value to collectors.

FAIRGROUNDS AND CIRCUS LOTS

Almost all towns and cities at one time or another had an area designated for the fairgrounds. In my home town of Lufkin, Texas, I yearly attended the fair from the time I was six until I was eighteen years of age. My parents said these fairgrounds were used for approximately twenty years prior to that. Before then, the fairgrounds were located in a different place, closer to the present main part of town. These are always excellent places to search, but be extra thorough around them because most coins—at least the ones of older vintage—are buried deeply. Four to seven inches are quite common depths for these old coins. If you can find an old-timer ask him where the concessions, the midway, and all of the coin-pitch tents were located. These will be the "hot spots" for you to search. Try to locate the gate where tickets were purchased. It is also a good idea to search the parking lots. In the event there is only a field left now with no one to testify as to where these places were located use some criss-cross method to try to locate the "hot spots".

In the good old days many circuses came to town and pitched their big tops at fairground sites or vacant lots. Many coins have been lost at these places since kids and grownups alike sat on the circus benches and became overly excited as the circus people and animals performed. It will pay you to try to locate these sites as did one treasure hunter. He chanced to discover an old publication which listed pre-1900 fairground sites all over the United States. He has found a bonanza in old coins on these locations, most of which were plowed fields or grazing lands at the time he hunted on them. I wonder if there are also publications that list locations of old city parks, state parks, CCC camps, old settlers' campgrounds, drive-in theaters, revival meeting places, circus locations, railroad depots, stage stops, baseball fields, race tracks, airports, *etc.*

PARKING AREAS

For some reason people always seem to lose coins when they get in and out of cars, so any area where cars have been parked is a likely place for coins to be found.

SIDEWALKS AND BUS STOPS

Wherever people walk, they lose coins. Search along all sidewalks. Be especially thorough at intersections or corners where people stop to wait for traffic. Grassy areas at intersections always yield a few coins or tokens. Check around benches at bus stops; if there are no benches remaining try to visualize where they might have been.

PARKING METERS

When searching around parking meters, especially in downtown grassy areas, be extremely careful not to leave any trace of your probing and digging. To search successfully directly adjacent to the parking meter pole, use the detector operating technique described in Chapter XX.

SCHOOLYARDS AND COLLEGES

Don't make the mistake of thinking that kindergarten schoolyards will yield only a few pennies. I have been successful in locating larger denomination coins, such as quarters, on playgrounds of elementary schools. Almost all areas around schools will be productive. Search first around sidewalks, trees, and playground equipment. I recall when I was in Kurth Elementary School in Lufkin, Texas, we would march over to the high school at lunchtime and form a long line outside the cafeteria door . . . the area was grassy, and even though I have not returned to search this area I would guess there are many coins awaiting some coin hunter.

Let your imagination be your guide. Better yet, if you are able to observe children while they are in school you can go well prepared at the earliest opportunity to search the areas where coins are most likely to be found.

College campuses are productive sites. No matter how old we are, we still lose money. College students are no exception. These students sit and lie on the campus grass more than do junior high or high school kids. They have more time between classes. They sit or lie down to rest, eat, talk, study —and lose coins and other paraphenalia.

CHURCHES

Not all coins carried to church are placed in the collection plate! They somehow find their way outside to the dirt and grass. Always check out your local churches. Grassy areas along walks and around steps are always good producers. Likewise, always search areas where cars pull in to unload passengers. If the ground is not paved you can expect to find coins that latecomers lose as they leap from their cars, or coins that fall from little hands as children try to hold on to Bibles, toys, and sometimes umbrellas.

WISHING WELLS AND CISTERNS

Probably most wishing wells are thoroughly and periodically cleaned out by their owners. However, if you are lucky enough to locate an occasional wishing well which has grass around where people stand, you will find coins they accidentally drop as they reach into their pockets for coins to throw into the well. Children are also quite good at dropping coins they intend to toss into the well.

Many times old schools and community playgrounds had cisterns or wells. People could come up and draw a bucket of drinking water. Often coins were thrown into these wells for luck. Perhaps in the process coins were lost on the ground. Many of these wells and cisterns had overhead roofs for shading. Naturally, this protection on hot or rainy days provided people with shelter and a place to congregate or sit down — and lose coins. There is a very old school cistern with overhead roof still standing in Centralia, Texas . . . I haven't searched it! It is located fifty yards south of the southern Centralia highway sign.

45

Between the two trees once stood the entrance of the United Methodist Church of Dickerson-Poolesville, Maryland. The church was torn down, moved, and reestablished in Dickerson in 1929. The site in the center of the picture yielded to Hunter Pritchard some 70 coins, all prior to 1927. Church lawns often yield a bonanza of coins. Photo courtesy A. T. Evans, Odessa, Texas.

Wayne Garrett, author's father, searches for coins around an old deserted church. Thanks to Mr. Garrett's vivid recollections of his early years, many lucrative, 60 years and older coin and treasure hunting sites are being worked by Mr. Garrett and his three sons.

46

NEWSPAPERS

Keep your eyes peeled as you read the newspapers. Quite often during excavation work or house-wrecking activities coins will be found. They will be found in walls of old houses and beneath the piers and foundations. Frequently bulldozers and other earth-moving equipment will dig up caches of coins, and this happening will be publicized in the papers. Find out where these places are and go out with your metal detector. Chances are, many of the coins and valuables will still be lying around the site.

As you get into the habit of daily scanning the newspapers don't forget the "lost and found" columns. Many people who lose valuable jewelry offer rewards. These instances could be golden opportunities for you to make additional money by recovering their lost objects. Also, your "deed" could easily be reported in the newspaper which might result in your being contacted by people requesting your help in locating their grandfather's lost money or some such valuables.

As you read the newspaper watch for announcements of locations of outdoor parties and gatherings. Knowledge of these spots could become valuable to the coin hunter.

SLOT MACHINE TOKENS

When I was in junior high school, my parents operated a furniture store located on North Main in Lufkin, Texas. The rear section of the old building was utilized as a storage area because portions of the flooring had been torn out. One day while I was cleaning up some old lumber I found a silver-dollar-sized token in the dirt. When I asked my father about it, he recalled that when he was a teenager the back part of the building was a gambling casino. One day several lawmen came into the casino and tore the place apart, hacking "one-armed bandits" and other fixtures into pieces. Thus ended the life of the casino, but somehow hundreds of metal gambling and slot machine tokens became lost in the dirt beneath the floor. I spent several days "getting rich" (and grimy) in the dirt in the back of that old store. Hopefully, this story will help some of you to locate "hot spots" of this type. Surely, there are many similar locations that still exist throughout the country.

ONCE A YEAR

All across the United States in many towns and cities there are ethnic groups such as Germans, Irish, Czechs, Poles, Scots, *etc.*, who make it a habit to get together yearly in parks or certain areas to hold their celebrations and festivities.

47

Bob Podhrasky, Chief Engineer, Garrett Electronics, tests the Master Hunter VLF/ TR Deepseeker, the forerunner of Garrett's ADS III, II and I detectors. A quick motion of the handle switch, to the left or right, electronically changes modes and retunes the instrument. Today's detectors are so advanced when compared to detectors of five years ago that coin hunting and treasure hunting are considered to be "renewed" hobbies. Areas thought to be completely worked out with yesterday's detectors are yielding bonanzas with today's new, supersensitive and sophisticated detectors.

One such case was brought to mind recently by Ed Bartholomew of Fort Davis, Texas. In a small town in one of the gold-mining Western states back during gold-rush days 5,000 people of German descent lived in this town. Once a year they all met at a certain crossroads to have a day-long get-together and all sorts of festivities. Much beer flowed on those days, and toward evening the spirits of most of the men were quite high. Consequently, without fail, the men began brawling, and a great deal of fighting and wrestling took place. The quantity of coins lost by these men is reported to be astronomical. The area has been worked for years now, and old coins are still being found.

Another story I heard recently . . . in a small town in one of the wheat states the townspeople had a yearly gathering and festivities day. One particular activity during the day was for youngsters. The townspeople piled up a huge stack of hay and threw thousands of coins of all denominations into the hay. At a given signal all the children could run, dive into the hay, and find money to their hearts' content. This went on for years. Naturally, when a coin hunter heard about it he inquired of the old-timers until he found the location of this activity. Yep, you guessed it. It was a true bonanza! Here is where research pays off. Understand what I mean?

There are many, many city and town coin hunting areas. Some not discussed in this chapter are included in Chapter V. Even yet the list is not complete.

THOSE FANTASTIC "TOPO" MAPS

United States Geological "Topo" maps are available to the public for a very small fee. These topographical maps are printed for almost every area in the United States. They are extremely precise in that they show roads, highways, cities, towns, and communities. The detail in these populated areas is fantastic. Houses (both occupied and unoccupied), barns, cisterns, wells, windmills, and other small landmarks are clearly shown and located. These maps are an absolute necessity in treasure and coin hunting. They are ideal for the beginning coin hunter because from these maps he can locate hundreds of possible coin hunting sites within a few miles of his home. A day or a weekend may be planned from these maps. To obtain complete information write one of the following addresses: (areas east of the Mississippi), Branch of Distribution, U.S.G.S., 1200 S. Eads, Arlington, Virginia 22202; (areas west of the Mississippi) Branch of Distribution, U.S.G.S., Box 25286, Denver Federal Center, Denver, Colorado 80225.

CHAPTER VII

Coin Hunting in the Country and While Traveling

TIPS WHEN TRAVELING

When traveling, it is always a good idea to leave early to allow extra time for coin hunting along the way. There are many places along all highways that can prove very profitable. Along Interstate 20, for instance, between Dallas and Odessa, Texas, eight drive-in theaters can be seen. Three of these are still active; five are deserted and in ruins. Three of the five are very old, and I would guess there are many coins in these fields with numismatic value equivalent to the cost of a good metal detector. Deserted highway stops and cafes, roadside parks, camping, hunting and fishing parks can be found along many highways. Stops such as these can prove not only very profitable, but they also give you a chance to stretch your legs or walk the dog.

As you travel you will pass through many towns and suburbs. Most of these have city parks, playgrounds, and swimming areas. Drive to the parks and let the kids play while you search the most likely places for rare coins. Don't forget to fill your holes, pick up and dispose of all trash you encounter or dig up. This will help calm the caretaker who just caught you digging up his grounds. Always stop at historical markers. Most travelers stop here, rest, photograph the marker . . . and lose coins. Who knows! You might dig up a treasure cache like the many which have been reported found around prominent historical and state border markers.

KIDS WILL PLAY

One type of place which should always be searched is any hilly or small cliff area in playgrounds and parks. Kids are drawn like magnets to small hills or cliffs where they can run and play, jump off and climb up again. My family loves to travel in the mountains, and when we stop at roadside parks and campgrounds in these regions the children always make a bee-line for little hills to play. I'm certain they've lost coins themselves.

In your hometown or other places with which you are familiar be on the look-out for motorcycle ramps and hills where motorcyclists enjoy trying their skills, racing up

50

This old drive-in theater has coins, character and many romantic memories. Don't you wish it could talk!

There are many old deserted cafes such as this one along our major highways and in our cities. Many old and rare date coins are being found at places like this. Generally, the coin hunter has failed to search these areas, but is now learning that many coins have been lost, especially in the parking areas and near the doors of cafes and other places where change is given to the customer as he leaves the place of business.

51

and down "popping wheelies". Also, you may remember areas where you as a kid used to hop aboard a cardboard slide or snow sled and go scooting down a steep embankment. I can recall two or three such places where I grew up. These places are always good for coins, knives, and other things children carry with them. While you are at it, take along a piece of cardboard to see how young you are. After all, metal detectors are really adult toys, the same as guns, bows and arrows, golf clubs, toboggins, and the like. If you think you are too old for this type of childish endeavor, what are you doing with a metal detector anyway!

BACK ROADS

In travel, the further you can get off the beaten path, the more likely you are to find old settlements and places where coin hunting is good. Why not check the map before you head out the next time? Look for alternate routes. Take the back roads sometimes. Instead of crowding the speed limit drive a little slower. You'll be amazed at how comfortable and relaxed you'll be at a slower rate of speed, and how much you'll enjoy the scenery and things you've never been able to in the past because your time was occupied in fighting the wheel at top speeds. You'll find many valuable coins around old courthouses and community recreational areas in some of the small, off-the-road towns.

Of course, you will need leads. You will need to talk to people who are familiar with these little towns and who can direct you to the parks, old campgrounds, peddlers' stands, fairgrounds, and so on. There are always some old-timers sitting around on the park benches or on the downtown city streets. Fred Mott of Dallas says the best way to approach these old fellows is to walk up to them and say, "Hello! Do you know where I can find any old-timers?" Of course, this always makes them feel good, even if they are pushing 100. It gets all of you in a laughing mood, and quite often these older people will think you are the greatest, a "lost grandchild", and will open their hearts to you. This is one method treasure hunters can use in researching. Fred has found this to be a way to pull information out of these storage vaults that no other means might allow. And too, don't forget to ask the old-timer his secret of longevity!

WRONG ROAD

What? You took the wrong turn! Don't fret. It is easy, and I know from experience, to become quite disturbed if a wrong road is taken. Don't despair. Just calm down, and

Charlie Weaver and Roy Lagal warm up by searching in this Nez Perce Indian reservation park located near Winchester, Idaho. Note the hoe that Roy Lagal is using to penetrate the snow and frozen ground. Charlie is using a specially designed pick slightly smaller than Roy's.

remember that you have no choice but to continue driving until you get back to your previous route. Take the opportunity to learn about a new section of town or country. Benefit from your extra driving. Don't complain about it. Who knows? You may find one or more excellent places to coin hunt that you might never have found had you not taken that wrong road.

RURAL MAILBOXES

Thanks to A. T. Evans for this tip. When searching in the country, don't forget to search around all rural mailboxes, especially those on little-used, back-country roads. For years and years rural dwellers put coins in the mailbox, along with letters to be picked up by the mail carrier. The coins were left in the boxes not only to pay for stamps which they hoped the postman would place on their letters, but also to purchase extra stamps and perhaps, occasionally, to tip the postman. Often, when the postman pulled letters out of the box, some coins slid out with them and were lost in the sand and dirt around the mailbox. One coin hunter filled a small tin can with Indianhead cents taken from around these back-country mailboxes.

My brother, Don, is a rural mail carrier in Angelina County, Texas. I asked him if people still place coins in

53

rural mail boxes. "Oh, yes," he replied, "Quite often people leave a few coins in the mail boxes with a note telling me they want to buy things like stamps and envelopes." So, coin hunter, if you find old and deserted farm homes or sites, try to visualize where the mail box may have been and search the area. You may fill your own tin can with Indianhead cents! Remember, however, tampering with the U. S. mail is a federal offense, so before searching around any active mailboxes always get permission from the land-owner. Offer him one-half of what you find.

PICNIC AREAS AND ROADSIDE PARKS

These are favorite places of the coin hunter. Search carefully around all tables and benches and out away from the tables, especially in grassy areas. If there are hand-rails where children can swing and loop-the-loop be espe-cially thorough in your search along these rails and out to approximately two feet on both sides. Search around the drinking fountain, along trails and around trees. Frequently, after eating people wander off into grassy areas to lie down for a quiet rest. If the areas are large, search the places that are shady. Search where cars are parked.

Don't miss the chance to search an old park like this one. Search carefully around posts, tables, and under the old trees where children dearly love to play. At the back edge of this park a trail leads off into the woods. Such trails should be searched, not only for lost coins but for other artifacts as well.

54

OLD CAMP GROUNDS AND FRESH WATER SPRINGS

These are excellent places to coin hunt, as well as to search for lost and purposely-hidden caches. Many lost caches or family deposits have been found around such areas. At night, when the wagon train or the campers stopped, families sometimes hid their wealth by burying it in the ground. Occasionally, due to Indian raids or other factors, these caches were never recovered. Search all old trails to and from camping grounds. Coins are quite often found around old springs, especially in the water. Here is a place where an underwater search loop is an absolute requirement. If you are considering the purchase of a detector I strongly encourage you to purchase one with submersible loops ("waterproof" may not mean "submersible"). If the encampment sites were near a river carefully search the banks both up and down from the place where the river was crossed. Recently, my brother, George, (Mom and Dad reared three boys) found a beautiful pair of silver scissors at an old ford on the Neches River near Lufkin, Texas. These scissors had a cross carved on both sides of the upper handles, and the maker's name (in German) was inscribed. These are worth a high price on the antique collectors' market.

These two men, Clyde and Tom Southern, Dade City, Florida, inspect some of the many coin and jewelry recoveries they have made in shallow swimming areas. Notice the abundance of rings and jewelry items that indicates the desirability of searching around swimming areas.

55

SWIMMING HOLES AND BEACHES

These are the areas in which more rings, charm bracelets, and other doo-dads will be found than any other place. Sometimes, as many rings and other items of jewelry are lost here as are coins. Be thorough in your search, and by all means let your search extend out into the water. Probably HALF the objects that are lost around swimming areas are lost in the shallow water. If you get a reading when scanning in the water with your detector, mark the location by placing your foot over the "hot spot". Then with a shovel bent at a 90-degree angle (holes should be drilled into the shovel to allow the water to drain out), reach down into the water and scoop up the mud under your foot. Slowly bring it to the surface and sift through it, being on constant alert for broken glass. Because of the enormous quantity of things lost in water a special section on suction dredging around swimming areas is included later in the book.

When searching on a sandy beach, you can in many cases do a good job with sieves and wire scoops. Scoops can be dragged along down to a depth of a few inches to recover all solid objects which will not pass through the size of wire

Note the specially-formed scoop that allows this coin hunter to scoop up the ground where his detector gave a metallic indication. The sides of the scoop allow him to retain everything he scoops up. He then picks out the metallic objects.

This coin hunter specializes in searching old swimming areas. Such locations have proved to be very good coin and jewelry hunting spots. He searches in water to a depth of two-and-a-half feet. Notice the length of the shovel. This permits him to reach into the water to scoop up the detected object as deeply as the detector can be submerged.

you have selected. It is best to build your sieve out of one-half-inch wire mesh which can be purchased at most lumberyards and hardware stores. I have a very efficient three-foot-square sieve I use not only for sifting sand in swimming and beach areas but also for sifting where fire has destroyed homes. It is constructed of 2"x4" lumber and half-inch wire mesh.

FISHING CAMPS

These may yield coins, especially if they are also camping areas. Coins will be lost from the pockets of persons who camp and sleep here. Much fishing tackle and many lead weights will be found, but be extra careful of those sharp fish hooks—they can be quite painful. In searching fishing camps, try to search out into the water where fishermen load and unload or get in and out of their boats. I found a .22 rifle under two feet of water near a boat launching area. The rifle was in excellent shape even though it had been lost several months because apparently it fell into the water with the open end of the barrel straight down. Mud was forced up into the barrel, sealing and preventing water from running into the barrel and into the riflings to cause rust. Fishing tackle, fishing boxes, and other equipment will be found here. *Caution:* Never wade out into any swimming or fishing areas without wearing good protective shoes. Broken glass abounds on the bottoms of these places. Be very careful when reaching down into the water to retreive your find. I suggest you use small rakes or a shovel with holes drilled into it to recover your finds. *Double Caution:* If you ever find a gun, check to see if it is loaded with ammunition! They usually are!

BRUSH ARBORS AND SOME SLEEPY FELLA

Do not fail to search thoroughly any area which in times past used to be a brush arbor. A brush arbor is an outdoor meeting place, generally where church was observed. Sawdust was used as a floor, and long benches were used for the people to sit on. For protection from the sun or light rain an overhead brush roof was built. Many valuable coins are found in these areas, and Bill Mahan tells why: "Can't you just imagine some sleepy fellow sitting on the hard benches, trying to stay awake to pay attention to the sermon being preached. He gradually drifts off to sleep, however, but is poked in the ribs when the collection plate is passed. He embarrassedly reaches into his pocket to pull out a few coins and drop them in the plate. Without his knowing it he drops a few to the ground to be quickly and quietly lost in the sawdust."

CHURCHES AND THE OLDEST NICKEL

One of the oldest nickels I have ever recovered was found five feet from the front doorstep of an old church. This nickel was found at a depth of five inches. It gave an excellent signal in our mineral-free East Texas dirt. When searching around churches, look especially in front of the church where adult church members are most likely to walk to following the sermon and stand talking to one another. Handerchiefs are pulled from pockets, and people fumble coins in their pockets. It has been proved many times that coins are lost here. Also search around the rear steps and old trees where children may have played. Quite often old churches had two outhouses. The ground surrounding and beneath these old places should be searched. Search areas where people would have parked cars or buggies; coins will be found there. Old churches also had their picnic areas. Make an attempt to locate and search them.

GHOST TOWNS

When searching ghost towns, some of the better places to look are underneath the boardwalks (or former boardwalk sites if they can be located), out in the streets and thoroughfares, and at the sites of salons, general stores, banks, and other money-handling establishments. Sometimes it is very difficult to determine the actual street locations, but there is one method that may be helpful.

As you know, most old ghost towns and early-day settlements had dirt streets which turned into mud streets at the slightest hint of rain. No one likes mud, even early-day settlers. In an attempt to improve their streets the townspeople hauled in fill material, such as rock that might have been recovered during mine digging or tunneling. This fill material quite often was high in iron ore content which can be detected by a detector. If you will criss-cross the area in which you believe a ghost town once existed, perhaps you may be able to determine the difference in iron ore content between the streets and other areas. Once you have located the streets it would be a simple matter to locate the boardwalks, houses, and other buildings or places that did not have the fill but might contain coins.

FIRES

In the early days fires were quite common. For example, the town of Cripple Creek, Colorado, was nearly wiped out by a fire. The city rebuilt upon the ruins. If you want to take the time to find the site of burned buildings it might pay you dividends. Searching the locations of burned buildings and houses sometimes can produce

While searching an old yard and house for coins and relics, Frank Angona came across this money hoard. It consisted of Mexican currency and coins. Frank said that while the cache wasn't of much monetary value, the excitement he experienced made the find worthwhile!

These old bronze and silver Roman coins, plus the Roman gravestone and the broken amphora were found by Richard Blondis at the site of an old castle. The items were found around the castle shown in the picture. Photos by Polner.

many coins. Often clumps of coins that are melted together will be found. The method used above to locate streets that were filled with mine tailings and other mineralized rock composition can be used to locate homesites. Quite often charred wood and other mineral composition that results from high temperatures during a fire will become conductive. Thus, you can readily locate the burned-over sites. San Francisco burned many years ago. Modern-day treasure hunters are reporting some valuable coins, tokens and other collectables at vacant lot sites, etc.

(Metal detectors sometimes perform extremely erratically when searching the location of a former fire because of the high carbon content of the debris and because there are usually many nails and other pieces of metal present in the soil.)

Discussed below are several actual locations where TH'ers have found a large quantity of coins. These are listed to give you some ideas that may help you find good coin hunting locations on your own.

KARL VON MUELLER

Karl von Mueller sends these location ideas. When the tourist-stop known as "Two Gun, Arizona" (east of Flagstaff) burned, over 2,000 coins were found by two coin hunters in the parking area months after the fire. A beginning coin hunter who purchased a detector at Exanimo in Segundo, Colorado, had beginner's luck and found over $60.00 in rings, brooches and bracelets along the waterfront of the Colorado River at Lake Havasu City, Arizona. Coin hunters with detectors often find numerous coins under the high bridge across the Rio Grande River west of Taos, New Mexico. Tourists toss coins into the River from the lookouts, and due to prevailing winds most of the coins land on the bank of the river and not in the water. Many coins can be found by sight alone, but a detector is needed for complete retrieval.

BOB PARKER

Just below Lake Havasu, Arizona, at Parker, Arizona, Bob found nearly $100 face value in old coins around a railroad depot and the old shipping pen area.

ROY LAGAL

Roy Lagal, Lewiston, Idaho, reports that one of his coin finding areas is along the right of ways where wrecking crews have torn down old buildings and houses in order to make way for new streets and highways. Roy also states that some of his best coins and coin cache finds have resulted when he was at construction sites where bulldozers were operating. He further states that these mechanical "big boys" do all the work for you, and sometimes you need only to go along behind one of these earth-moving machines and use your eyes.

ONLY A SMALL PORTION

The locations we have just discussed actually represent only a small portion of the good coin hunting places available to you. Certain activities went on in some parts of the country and not in others. Industries differed. Recreational pursuits varied in different parts of the country. I am certain that as you drive around and search different areas and talk with old-timers you will discover new locations. Your available time is the only limiting factor.

L. L. "Abe" Lincoln displays a few of his most valuable coins. Many of them are gold coins which he found while searching around 100-year-old Idaho gold mining camps. "Abe" has been very successful in all phases of treasure hunting.

This man, Mr. J. B. Estes, is a very successful, full-time treasure and coin hunter. He is standing in front of his home on wheels, a specially equipped small step-van. He is holding one of his rare coins, an 1825 rim half-dollar. He has found countless thousands of coins, including several big caches of large cents, Indianhead pennies, and buffalo nickels.

The author found this stone "coin" (?) while he was searching for Indian relics in West Texas. The "coin" is almost perfectly round and is very nearly the size, shape, and thickness of a nickel.

CHAPTER VIII

Hidden Bounty on the Beaches

For hundreds of years people have flocked to the beaches in search of pleasure, fun, and respite from problems of everyday life. Most come to lie in the sun and splash in the surf. Another group has been coming to the beaches for entirely different reasons. They seek lost treasure: coins, rings, watches and other jewelry lost by the modern-day sun bather. These treasure seekers are also searching for the gold and silver coins, ingots and artifacts which originally were part of the cargoes of many wrecked ships which have found their final resting places amid the shallow offshore coastal waters. The fortunes awaiting these treasure hunters and coin hunters is estimated in the millions of dollars.

SPANISH TREASURE

Silver pieces-of-eight, commonly discovered on Texas and Florida coasts, are a real find for the coin hunter. Sometimes they are found individually; sometimes they are found in bunches or clumps. These pieces of pirate money, usually called "cobs", get their name from the Spanish *cabo de barra*, or "end of the bar". The cobs were clipped in succession from the end of a strip of silver. After being trimmed to the proper weight, they were placed between two iron or steel dies into which designs for the cobs had been engraved. When forcefully struck, the dies were driven into the metal to produce the finished coin. Silver during this period was minted in denominations of one-half, 1, 2, 4, and 8 *reales*. The 2 and 4 *real* pieces became known as "two bits" and "four bits". A *real* had a value of about 12½ cents. Cobs, as well as any silver coins that have laid beneath the sea and sand for years, are not the bright, shiny specimens found illustrated in coin guides. The chemical action of the salt water and air turn the coins into unrecognizable, blackened pieces of metal which must be cleaned in order to restore them to their "new" condition. Those unfamiliar with this sea water corroding process may walk right past such coins as they lie exposed on the beach. Alert beachcombers can spot the black coins with the aid of a metal detector.

There are many Spanish galleon locations off the Florida mainland and along the Keys. One such area falls

When a treasure hunter becomes successful in one phase of treasure recovery, naturally he or she has a desire to try various other forms of treasure hunting. Bill Bosh started coin hunting in Idaho parks. His success then led him into cache hunting. Success there led him into many parts of the U.S. in the search for other money caches. Then, when the Australian gold rush hit...yep, you guessed it...he took off for the Outback in Western Australia where he found more than $100,000-worth of gold! What is he doing now? It is plain to see in the above photograph that he has turned his attention to the swimming beaches! With the introduction of Garrett's Sea Hunter underwater detectors, Bill is now using his XL500 to find gold and silver rings, watches, and multitudes of coins, as you can see from the treasure he found searching this beach! Keep it up, Bill! What's next?

65

within a span of coastline just below Cocoa Beach, beginning at a point near the town of Sebastian, extending some 35 miles down the east coast to a spot just south of Fort Pierce. This location has been determined to be the watery grave of a fleet of eleven, 1715, treasure-laden vessels that were bound from Havana to Spain carrying a cargo reportedly valued at more than fourteen million dollars. A violent hurricane sank all the ships but one and took the lives of hundreds of sailors. Immediately following the hurricane, six million dollars in cargo was recovered. The remainder lay undisturbed until the 1940's when Kip Wagner and a friend found and identified several silver coins. Consequently, Real Eight Corporation was formed. The amount of wealth recovered by this group at this site and others is reported to be more than twenty million dollars, and work is continuing. Much Spanish and additional treasure is still abundant along the Florida, Texas, and other coasts.

TODAY'S TREASURES

Thus far we have discussed primarily Spanish wrecks, making little mention of modern-day lost treasure. Any public beach, whether of an ocean or lake, is a good place to try your luck. In most cases, luck you will have! Provided another coin hunter hasn't beaten you there. Sun bathers and swimmers lose coins, rings, watches, medallions, and all kinds of jewelry in countless numbers. It is easy to understand why. Take rings, for instance. People go swimming, play in the water, or run and are active on the beach in hot sun. They perspire and slosh on greasy sun tan lotion. If they are wearing rings, the rings can slip off their fingers. As people swim and make strokes in the water, throw balls, or generally run and engage in horseplay with one another, rings slip off their fingers and fall to the ground to become quickly mashed into the sand by foot traffic. Usually when people lose rings on the beaches they have no idea when or where they lost them. The same is true for other jewelry . . . necklaces, medallions, watches, and so on. Many people carry coins loose in bathing suit or beach jacket pockets. These coins can quite easily fall out and be lost.

The best time to look for modern-day coins in a beach area is immediately after the weekend or any time after crowds have been there. The best time to look for pieces-of-eight is immediately after a heavy rainstorm or hurricane. Not only will the coins become uncovered on the beach, but coins that have laid under shallow water will be picked up and hurled upon the beach. If you visit the beaches make

Underwater archaeologist Bob Marx has probably logged in more hours searching for historical and shipwreck treasures than any other treasure hunter. There are very few islands, harbors, and ocean areas where Bob has not been in his quest for treasure and knowledge. Spanish shipwrecks are his specialty, and he long ago lost count of the value of the treasure he has recovered. He works closely with underwater archaeological groups the world over to locate and excavate the countless thousands of "lost" historical sites. He has written twenty-seven books, the latest of which is ROBERT MARX: QUEST FOR TREASURE, published by Ram Publishing Company. (See page 208.) Marx's book is a true story of his discovery and salvage of a 1656 king's Spanish treasure galleon which sank near the Bahamas. The book is an absorbing account of Marx's unrelenting effort and the methods he used to bring up millions in treasure from the ocean floor.

Because the majority of detectors are likely to be used 95% of the time for coin hunting, certain detector models are designed and built to be the most efficient for this particular aspect of treasure hunting. Detection characteristics, mechanical configuration and balance, great depth on coins, ease of handling, and almost total freedom from controls adjustment are the advance design features found on a new breed of coin hunting instrument, the Freedom 2 Coin Commander. The Freedom 2 is the result of a new concept in detector design which reflects a complete departure from conventional ideas.

it your business to learn the known productive areas. Padre Island, off the Texas coast, is known for a large quantity of Spanish cobs that have been recovered. There are even reported finds of original 100 pound Spanish copper containers that were filled with the treasured coins. Padre Island, however, has been placed "off limits" to metal detectors because it is a National Seashore under control of the National Park System.

IN WHAT CONDITION WILL THEY BE FOUND?

Most gold items remain fairly well in like-new condition for long periods of time. Gold is generally impervious to the chemical action of salt water. Silver in almost all cases turns black after only a few months of beach exposure. Copper coins sometimes turn green as they slowly corrode. Inexpensive cheaply-plated medallions and similar artifacts will very quickly deteriorate—so quickly, in fact, that after about two or three months they will have been eroded completely away.

Roy Lagal scans a swimming beach with his Master Hunter. With one swift stroke of his hoe he can retrieve most coins. Shortly after this picture was taken, Charlie Weaver and Charles Garrett completed the job by using a suction dredge to clean out the swimming area. Across the Snake River is a portion of Lewiston, Idaho. Roy reports that most coin and treasure hunters are changing to the discriminating pulse induction and VLF types in order to achieve the depth and ground elimination needed to reach the deeper, older coins.

WHERE TO SEARCH

On an open beach one place might be just about as good as another. Sunbathers and swimmers and those who just watch are active all the way from shallow water areas back up into the limits of the beach or park. It's best, if you can, to observe swimmers, sunbathers, and on-lookers on a crowded day. From such observations you will be in a better position to find the "hot spots". Always search around concession stands, piers, lifeguard towers, drinking fountains, and locations of this sort where people congregate.

On some beaches there are roped off areas designated for swimming. By all means, search these places first. It's a good idea to strike up a conversation with, perhaps, the lifeguard or the concession stand operators. It may be that the swimming areas of by-gone days were located elsewhere on the beach. You would certainly want to search those sites. Also, lifeguards may know where rings and valuables are reported to have been lost. Try working along the water's edge at both low and high tides. Both could be profitable. You will encounter much less trash near the water, but remember some very valuable coins and jewelry have been found back away from the beach in the heavy traffic areas.

DETECTOR OPERATION ON THE BEACH

Many detector operators experience difficulty when operating their detectors on the beach until they learn a few basic rules. On some beaches black magnetic sand is found, either in stringers, clumps, or in solid patches spread out over large areas. Black magnetic sand is "negative" mineral.

Pulse induction convertible land/sea detectors with trash elimination are the choice of most beach hunters. The pulse will ignore wetted salt and magnetic black sand; is extremely easy to use; and it will detect coins, rings, and jewelry to extreme depths.

To operate a pulse induction detector simply turn the instrument on and adjust the audio for threshold (minimum) audio sound. Then begin searching. No ground adjustments are needed. Simply dial in the amount of metal trash elimination you want.

Fresh water beach hunters often choose VLF types. In salt water areas where there is no magnetic sand, beachcombers are having excellent success using VLF detectors in the trash elimination mode. At the approximate trash elimination point where bottle caps are eliminated from detection, salt water is also eliminated. When scanning on a dry beach and you scan out into salt water, you won't notice any change in detector audio threshold. You can expect excellent depth with quality VLF discriminating detectors.

These silver and gold coins, the two gold bars, and the gold cross were found just off the coast of Texas by an underwater archaeological research team of the Texas Antiquities Committee. They recovered thousands of priceless treasures and relics from four Spanish ships which were driven into shallow Texas waters and destroyed by a hurricane in 1552. You may write the Texas Antiquities Committee, P. O. Box 12276, Capitol Station, Austin, Texas 78711, to obtain on loan a 16 mm film (prepared by the State of Texas) which documents this historical recovery. Demonstrated in the 35-minute film are scientific methods employed to recover, clean, and preserve anchors, cannon barrels, and other valuable artifacts.

This treasure hunter prepares to search in three feet of water with his specially rigged underwater five-inch Garrett BFO search coil. Note the special scoop he has built to aid in his recovery work.

This is a close-up of a special floating metal detector and recovery apparatus. Notice the scoop; the detector rigidly mounted so it cannot fall into the water, but yet mounted so it can be operated quite easily by one person; the special handle; and the box where the goodies are kept.

71

When utilizing a TR on the beach over black magnetic sand or wet sand, generally only the scrub technique is successful. If you haven't already looked into the TR scrub technique study it and give it a try.

As you begin to search a beach for the first time these problems will become obvious. They can be overcome, however, quite easily, with patience and concentrated effort. Keep at it. Good results will be yours.

Master Sergeant Joe Maenner had above average coin hunting luck while he was stationed at Fairchild Air Force Base in Spokane, Washington. He made a systematic search of Coeur D'Alene Beach and Rocky Point Beach. During one of his trips to Coeur D'Alene, someone told him of an old swimming beach near Post Falls, Idaho. The total of his finds at Post Falls beach is as follows: almost 2900 coins, ten wedding rings, twelve birthstone rings, 37 religious medals, and 16 assorted jewelry items. He said that the coins were so numerous that many of them were simply lying in view when the tides went out. He searched during the winter months, and sometimes the ground was frozen and snow was on the ground.

PROTECT YOUR INSTRUMENT

As a note of caution, sand on most beaches is quite fine, and is blown around through the air. Most persons who have operated on the beach have gone home, opened their instruments, and been able to pour out quantities of sand from the detector housing. With this thought in mind, you might want to carry along a plastic bag to slip over the detector housing. You may need to cut a hole for the tuner knob and speaker. It's a good way to protect your instrument against the elements. In the event you ever drop your detector in salt water, flush it out immediately with fresh water to wash out most of the salt and prevent or help reduce salt water corrosion. In any case, it is not likely that fresh water will do it any more damage.

EARPHONES

If you have ever searched along the beach you know that surf noises can be quite loud. So loud, in fact, that unless the detector volume has extra loudness capability you cannot adequately hear the detector's signals, and you must wear earphones. (You may also require earphones if you are working in other areas where there is high background noise, such as wind blowing through the trees or cultural noise such as automobile traffic.)

If you are using earphones here is a tip that will help you get more detection capability from your instrument.

72

Generally, when you wear earphones you must reduce detector volume. Otherwise, the volume would be so loud as to cause ear discomfort. With most detectors, especially the BFO when the volume is reduced in order to make earphones have the correct volume, the quality of the signal may be reduced. Harmonics you might need for the best detection can be lost. There is a way to prevent this reduction in signal quality. Use earphones that have individual earpiece volume adjustment. This will permit you to operate your instrument at a high volume setting with the panel volume control knob as you would use in normal speaker operation. You can then reduce the volume of sound coming from the earphones by adjusting each individual earpiece. In other words, turn the volume up high on the detector control panel and down low on the earphones. This method will prevent the loss of the much-needed high frequency harmonics and give you better detection capabilities when using earphones.

The metal detector is the best means available for locating coins, artifacts and valuable treasure site clues. In Chapter V you will find the beach and its good locations listed. Don't ever pass up an opportunity to visit beach areas in the search for coins. Not only is it fun and enjoyable, but, who knows what you may turn up!

Bob Jones and Frank Kearney eat an early breakfast before getting out on the sands of Padre Island to search for the pieces of eight that are commonly found three miles above Mansfield Pass. Apparently a treasure-laden Spanish ship went down off the coast near here because many Spanish coins and artifacts are found at this site. The Padre Island National Seashore is now closed to all treasure hunters.

CHAPTER IX

How to Dig That Coin and Tools You'll Need

DON'T use a screwdriver — use a knife to retrieve coins. A screwdriver when used as a prybar will scratch the coins. DON'T use a knife for coin hunting . . . use a screwdriver. The knife will destroy the sod. DON'T use a coin probe; it will scratch your coins. *DO* use a probe in order to pinpoint your coins so that you do the least damage to the sod. Sounds confusing, doesn't it? Well, it is, unless you understand for what type of soil these suggestions were given.

I am sure most of you have read the suggestions given by many coin hunters as to how to dig and retrieve coins. If you have paid attention you have noticed that often the suggestions seem to contradict each other. The problem is that each type of soil requires, generally, a different digging and retrieval technique. Retrieving coins from the beach, of course, is perhaps the easiest. Retrieving coins from hard-packed dry clay soil with a heavy growth of, say, St. Augustine grass, is very difficult and requires an entirely different retrieval method. Retrieval in good, loose dirt, covered with, for example, Bermuda grass, lies somewhere in between the two above extremes. I have coin hunted perhaps in most types of soil, including frozen ground in some of the northern states. Thus, be assured that the techniques required are different, but must be learned by each coin hunter and applied appropriately for maximum efficiency.

COINHUNTERS EXPLAIN

Rather than write about the various recovery techniques myself, I wrote to several well-known treasure hunting personalities who live in different parts of the country and who are accustomed to digging in many different types of soils. I asked them to explain how they go about retrieving coins in soil peculiar to their areas or under special coin hunting conditions. My thanks to these coin hunters for supplying information and pictures that help tell the story.

You will note in reading through this chapter that several of the coin hunters use different methods in either probing or retrieving. Keep in mind these people have

Pamella Wendel, Seminole, Florida, is fortunate to live very close to many miles of good coin hunting beaches. She has collected thousands of coins, rings, and other jewelry that vacationers have left behind on nearby beaches.

Bill Smith is an extremely active coin and treasure hunter. He and Mrs. Smith have amassed more than 10,000 coins, more than 100 valuable rings, and a large assortment of other valuables.

worked out their own recovery techniques for speed, ease of recovery, less damage to coins and sod. One method which may work over one given type of sod may not be the best for another type. Study them all; practice them all; and select the method you prefer in the area you work.

THE WENDEL'S SAND

Bill and Pamella Wendel are fortunate to live very close to many miles of Florida coin hunting beaches. Many tourists come to Florida to enjoy the sandy beaches. While there, they lose coins, jewelry and other valuable objects. The Wendels have worked out a technique for the recovery of these objects. "In this loose beach sand recovery is easy, but yet there are a few tricks we have learned that help speed up our recovery. Generally, we use two tools, a wire mesh scoop-sifter and a small plastic trowel something like a sugar scoop. When we have pinpointed the metallic object with the detector, if the sand is loose and fine, we can make one pass through the sand with the sifter and recover the objects. When working along the wet, saturated sands near the water's edge, the sifter is difficult to use. There we use the trowel. We insert the trowel several inches into the ground and with one quick twist we can 'plug' the beach sand, remove the plug, and retrieve the coin." "I rarely do any digging with my hands," says Pamella, "because of the danger of glass, fish hooks, shells, and other sharp objects. I tried using gloves, but most of the time it is too hot for that. Coin hunting on the beach is really a great way for a person to enjoy his or her free time. In the right areas the rewards can sometimes be truly great. We use both the Garrett VLF and pulse induction detectors on the beach and out in the surf."

BILL SMITH'S HALF CIRCLE

Bill and Mrs. Smith have been coin hunting for many years and have amassed more than 10,000 coins, more than 100 valuable rings, and a large assortment of other valuables. Bill states that they have good soil conditions in his area, not too much mineral, and digging is pretty easy. He prefers headphones because with them he can hear the weaker signals and they keep most on-lookers from asking him questions. He says he loves to visit with people, but not while he is hunting coins. "After I have pinpointed a coin as closely as possible with the instrument, I cut a half-circle with a Pro-Digger three inches

76

deep. Then I fold the turf back, and if the coin is not in the plug I remove a second and deeper plug, making sure the loose dirt falls back into the hole. When I retrieve the coin, I fold the turf

Pamella Wendel has few rivals when it comes to total hours spent with metal detectors. For many years she and her family have been active in coin, treasure, and cache hunting; beachcombing; prospecting; nugget hunting; and dredging. She has traveled to Texas, Oklahoma, Missouri, Georgia, South Carolina and other states in search for treasure. As a result of her successes she has been written about in practically every treasure hunting book and periodical, as well as in ARGOSY's TREASURE HUNTING ANNUAL. My thanks to Pamella for sending this photograph of a few of her most valued finds. The extremely rare buttons shown date from about 1790 to 1835. Pamella has recently switched over to the deepseeking VLF/TR detector types to be sure of maximum depth detection. She doesn't want valuable treasures to go unfound.

back in place and step on it. I have found this to be the best method for the Bermuda grass areas we have in Oklahoma. If you cut a full circle in this grass it kills the roots. I never put trash back into the holes. It just means someone else will have to dig it up again. It's best to wear an apron with two pockets. Put the coins on one side and the trash on the other. Good luck!"

MIKE KRAMPTIZ

Mike Kramptiz is an active coin hunter from Connecticut. He makes most of the East Coast treasure hunts. If you attended any of the Search International treasure hunts, you probably saw him out hunting. When he wasn't participating in a hunt, he was always busy preparing and painting dozens of signs that were needed. He constantly works for the good of treasure hunting. He and Eric Lawson, assisted by Elaine Lawson, planned and put together an excellent slide presentation showing various methods of pinpointing and retrieving coins properly and the various tools coin hunters need. In the presentation, he recommends that, if you must cut a plug, you cut it square so that it will fit back into the hole perfectly. He recommends further that the plug be cut deeply, with lots of soil attached to it so the powerful lawnmowers don't pull the plug from the ground before the grass has become re-established. Cone-shaped plugs (pointed at the bottom) are more likely to be uprooted by mowers. Also, he suggests that you try to pinpoint the coin in the plug so that removal of the coin will be more precise and you won't have to break the plug apart to find the coin. The more dirt that can be left on the plug, the more likely the grass will live and re-root. See the end of this chapter for information on how to obtain a free loan of this fifteen-minute slide presentation that you can show to your club.

A GOOD SCREWDRIVER METHOD

A screwdriver is widely used for extracting coins. A well known East Coast coin hunter submitted this method and he says he can find, dig, and recover coins faster and better, with less damage, with a screwdriver than with any other tool he has used. Here is his method. After pinpointing the coin with the detector he pushes the screwdriver at a 45°-angle into the ground, about 5" deep and 2-3" in back of the pinpointed area. He uses a screwdriver with a dull point in case he accidentally makes contact with the coin. With the screwdriver inserted into the ground he pushes forward and to the left with the screwdriver, making a 3-5" long "slit" in the ground. Then he pulls the screwdriver back to its original position and shoves it forward again, but this time to the right. Thus he has cut two "slits" which form a V-shaped piece of sod. He pulls the V-shaped piece of sod forward with his hand, rotating it out of the

Twelve hundred treasure hunters search for thousands of dollars in coins and tens of hundreds of instant prize tokens. More than $100,000 in prizes was given away to entrants at this largest hunt ever held, the First Annual International Championship Treasure Hunt. This event was sponsored by the International Treasure Hunting Society, P.O. Box 3007, Garland, Texas 75041. Write for information or send name, address and $3 for first year's subscription to their very informative publication, THE SEARCHER.

Roy Gene Rolls, Forest Ranch, California, displays a few of his unusual finds made while searching an old California ghost town. Relics like these bring high prices on the collectors' market.

ground. "After you have retrieved your coin the sod will fall back into the hole in the exact place it came out, and the grass roots will not die. Also, the screwdriver does not cut the grass roots as the "V" is formed, but merely pulls most of the roots through the ground." He states that a park caretaker had much rather see a coin hunter with a screwdriver than with a knife.

ANOTHER SCREWDRIVER METHOD

One treasure hunter suggests a slightly different retrieval method to use in parks and other areas where the sod must not be greatly damaged. After pinpointing with the detector carefully insert a dull-pointed probe into the ground until you touch the coin. This gives its depth. Then insert a heavy duty screwdriver into the ground directly above the coin to a depth slightly less than the depth of the coin. Rotate the screwdriver gently until you have a cone-shaped hole about three inches in width across the top. It is then usually an easy matter to remove the coin with just a little hand or screwdriver point digging. This method requires some practice and skill, especially when probing, because the coin must not be scratched. To fill the hole, insert the screwdriver into the ground two or three times around the opening. With just a small pressure toward the hole the surrounding soil and grass fill it in, leaving no scar.

CHARLIE WEAVER'S PROBE

Charlie Weaver, of Lewiston, Idaho, uses a stainless steel probe with a diameter a little larger than the wire of a coathanger. The point is carefully rounded and smoothed so that it will not scratch a coin's surface. Charlie has been coin hunting for many years in Idaho, and has amassed a beautiful collection of coins, rings and other valuables which, he says, he must keep in the bank! I have watched Charlie coin hunt and retrieve his finds, and I must say that his method is a good one. It is exact, precise, and quick. He is very adept at pinpointing with his detector and then locating the coin with his probe. The following is a true story I witnessed myself. Charlie received a signal with his detector. He inserted the probe into the ground and touched the coin on his first probe insertion. He cut a cone-shaped plug, removed it from the ground, and there was the coin, a 1906-O quarter, near the bottom of his plug. He only had to reach over and take the coin with his fingers. Believe it or not, the quarter was buried four inches deep, standing vertically! Remember, I said the first time he inserted the probe he touched the coin. With the coin standing on edge, I would say that was a tremendous feat.

This is the 1906-0 quarter that Charlie Weaver located at four inches. As discussed in the chapter, HOW TO DIG THAT HOLE, Charlie's first probe insertion in the ground touched the edge of the coin. The pinpointing feat is especially remarkable in that Charlie was using very large searchcoils; This ability, however, comes after many, many hours of concentrated coin hunting effort.

Charlie says many people tell him he should not use his probe for locating the coin before he digs. They tell him he could scratch coins and ruin their value. "Of course, I scratched a few at first," relates Charlie, "but now I can tell instantly when I have first touched the coin with the probe and rarely do I ever scratch one. By probing first I can determine the exact depth and position of the coin. This method is precise, exact and gives me much speed. I insert the probe until I locate the coin. This tells me where it is and how deep. With my knife I cut a cone-shaped plug, and in most cases when I remove the plug the coin is located in the very bottom of the plug. Of course, sometimes I run into a tree root and occasionally a piece of glass, but I have learned pretty well to identify these objects when I touch them with the probe."

BILL FANGIO'S MANICURED LAWN

Bill Fangio, a man well known in electronics design, says that occasionally all treasure hunters will have the opportunity to search in an area that has a well-manicured lawn or in an area where no one is normally permitted to dig a hole. In these areas, however, there is a method which can be used that is acceptable to most lawn caretakers. It is a little slower than other methods, but it gets the job done. After pinpointing the coin with your instrument, carefully probe with a rounded point. After you have located the coin with the probe, insert a screwdriver with about an 8″ shaft approximately an inch or two out from the probe to a depth that places the tip of the screwdriver slightly below the tip of the probe. Remove the probe, and carefully work the object to the surface. This method is a little difficult to use, but with practice it becomes easier, and if you are not permitted to cut the grass you should learn how to do it. You might try experimenting by bending the end of the screwdriver out slightly, forming a small "scoop." In some types of soil this screwdriver scoop helps retrieve the coin. It's a lot harder to use this method than just cutting a plug out of the ground, but it is better to use it than to leave those old and valuable coins in the ground.

THERE ARE OTHER METHODS

Well, there you have it. Seven different methods of probing for and/or retrieving buried coins. There are other methods that can be used depending upon the soil condition. In extremely hard and sunbaked soil and in frozen ground it is necessary to use some type of wide-blade pick to actually hack your way into the ground. In softer ground the digging is easier, and one of the above methods or some variation of one of them might be more practical. Nevertheless, regardless of the type of ground, you should study these methods and work out the one or ones best suited to your needs. Remember, soil conditions change with the weather as well as the geography so study and practice all methods so that you will be well prepared. Good luck; happy digging! And . . . fill those holes!

TOOLS YOU'LL NEED

Your first and most important tool is a good metal detector. You can search in certain areas, especially along the beaches, without the use of a detector; however, in all areas, a detector will greatly multiply your take. Good metal detectors for coin hunting cost in the neighborhood of from $100-$300. The highest-priced detector is not necessarily the best coin hunting detector. It is possible that one type selling for $100 may be equal to or superior to another type selling for $300. Carefully review all manufacturers' published data and select the best instrument for your needs. Four good books to read and study if you are considering the purchase of a detector are: "HOW TO TEST" DETECTOR FIELD GUIDE, DETECTOR OWNER'S FIELD MANUAL, THE COMPLETE VLF-TR METAL DETECTOR HANDBOOK, and ELEC-TRONIC PROSPECTING.

Other useful tools are a locating probe, a knife, a screwdriver, a weed sickle, an apron with pockets for depositing your finds, a small flashlight for night searching, an old trash box, and — don't laugh, a lawnmower. You will soon learn you may require different types of digging tools for different types of ground conditions. A weed sickle or cutter is a handy item to have because quite frequently you will encounter bushes and clumps of grass you must remove in order to scan an area properly. If you search at night you must use a flashlight. The trash box is good to dump your found trash into if there are no trash containers available.

I'm not suggesting that each treasure hunter carry around a lawnmower in his trunk, but I would venture to guess the day is coming when you will gladly mow a church lawn or the lawn around an old house in order to search for lost coins, especially those from an early era.

NOTES

You may obtain a free loan of a very informative and in-structive 35 mm slide presentation with sound entitled AD-VANCED COIN RETRIEVAL. Proper coin pinpointing and re-trieval techniques are shown, as well as the best ways in which to retrieve coins in various soils without damaging the sod and different kinds of recovery tools. The presentation is ideal for treasure hunting club programs and similar gatherings. Write or contact Customer Service Department, Garrett Electronics, 2814 National Drive, Garland, Texas 75041 U.S.A. There is no charge for the loan of this and other films that Garrett makes available. You pay only for shipping and insurance both ways.

Similar material is also available as one of the Garrett series of instructional audio cassette tapes. Like the slide pre-sentation, entitled ADVANCED COIN RETRIEVAL, it may be purchased for a small amount from any Garrett dealer or ordered from the factory at the address given above.

CHAPTER X

Underwater Recovery with the Detector and Dredge

In this chapter I will present briefly both detector and suction dredge underwater recovery techniques. Many people are now utilizing their detectors and dredges to clean out swimming and recreational underwater sites. If you are fortunate enough to find one or more of these unworked locations your rewards should be great. It is estimated that more than one-half of the coins, rings, jewelry and other items lost at swimming areas and on beaches are lost in the water. Thus, persons using their detector along beaches should also search in the water, provided their instruments are equipped with submersible search coils. Generally, a detector operator with this type of instrument can search to a depth of more than two feet, but unless you have some type of special digging probe you are limited to arm's length searching.

My thanks to TREASURE MAGAZINE for permitting me to reprint portions of an article from the March 1973 issue of TREASURE (Vol. 4, No. 3). The pictures were taken at the 1972 Prospector's Club of Southern California meet at California City, California. I was fortunate to meet the man about whom the article was written, Wallace Chandler, and see firsthand the things he had found. The sight was truly astounding. I believe that after you have read this reprint your blood will be churning and you'll be ready to go!

"Wallace Chandler now lives in Lansing, Michigan, where he spends his free time coinshooting for rings, coins, and jewelry. But Wallace goes about it a little differently. He coinshoots the beaches all right, but he does it *below* the water line, not on the sand as most treasure hunters do.

"Chandler has been treasure hunting for a good many years now. He originally became interested in the hobby when he bought a detector to search for gold nuggets in California. But now he uses his detector back east for coinshooting beaches, parks, playgrounds, and fair grounds.

"One day Chandler saw another treasure hunter working *in* the water. 'I thought he was crazy. It was my belief that everything lost was lost on the beach. When the man came in, I asked him how he was doing. His reply was

Wallace Chandler and others look on as the author inspects some of the rings and jewelry found by Wallace during his many searches in the water as described in the accompanying article.

The close-up shows the construction details of Chandler's underwater scoop. Most of the holes are ⅜-inch in diameter. The old Army-type shovel was rotated to its 90-degree position and welded.

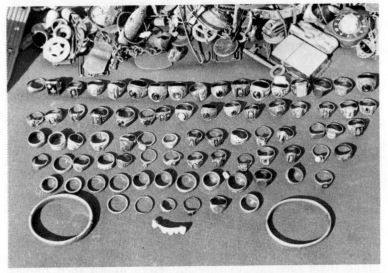

This is a close-up of a few of the many hundreds of rings Chandler has found during his underwater exploration activities. Note the false teeth bridge in the front center of the picture. Some swimmer went to the dentist that day!

'so-so', and he reached into his pocket and pulled out a handful of coins. He had a Franklin half-dollar, lots of other coins, and a couple of silver rings. After seeing that I started working the water also, and have been ever since!'

"Wallace Chandler's success has been phenomenal. In a single day he has found as many as 22 gold rings, 11 half-dollars, 32 quarters, 44 dimes, 53 nickels, and an uncounted number of pennies. On another day Chandler located 14 gold rings, 6 half-dollars, 30 quarters, plus a number of dimes and nickels. All from the same beach. And on still another day at another location he came up with four diamond rings.

"During the past five years that Chandler has been hunting below the water line, he has come up with between 4000 and 5000 rings, some 1500 of them being gold.

"While Chandler sells many of his finds, he keeps a couple of boxes of his favorites with him most of the time. Very few of these get sold.

" 'I have a friend who polishes and re-sets the stones if they need it,' Chandler explains. 'But you'd be surprised how many of the rings are found in really fine condition.'

"Chandler works the many public and private beaches and swimming areas throughout the midwest. 'Nearly any place where people swim will produce finds,' Chandler explains, 'but it is generally best in sheltered areas where there is not too much wave action or turbulence. . . .'

"Chandler uses a Garrett 'Scanner' metal detector. It is a specially-built, four-year-old model with submersible coils. I understand, however, that Garrett Electronics of Garland, Texas, now equips all Garrett instruments with submersible coils.

" 'I run the beat (the 'Scanner' is a BFO) just a little faster than 'slow' when I am working normal sand and gravel,' explains Chandler. 'But if I get into magnetic black sands I run the beat-note up a little faster.'

"To locate an underwater target, Chandler works slowly along the bottom with the detector's coil. When he gets a signal, he puts the toe of his boot where the center of the coil was. Then he starts four or five inches in front of the toe of his boot, and scoops back under his foot with a specially-built shovel he uses for his work.

"Chandler's shovel is a standard GI 'foxhole' shovel welded at 90 degrees and the handle extended to four-feet in length. Strips of metal are welded around the sides to make them one-half to three-quarters of an inch higher. Then the blade of the shovel is 'riddled' with $3/8$ inch holes.

"The holes are put in with an electric drill, and are

86

large enough to let sand and fine gravel flow through easily, but small enough to stop coins and rings. Chandler also uses a shovel with no holes for working in more compacted material such as mud.

"Some treasure hunters make up larger scoops about twice the size of Chandler's shovel, while others use a pitch fork with a sheet-metal nose and the bottom lined with screen or hardware cloth. The looser the material you are working, the larger the scoop needed.

" 'It's true, you do wind up with an awful lot of bottle tops and pull-tabs,' Chandler explains, 'but when the water is clear enough to see your feet, it helps cut down on a lot of the trash you would otherwise get. But trash or not, let me tell you, it's for sure the good stuff makes up for all the junk you find!' "

OTHERS HAVE SUCCEEDED

Roy Lagal and Charlie Weaver of Lewiston, Idaho, Rene LeNeve of Bloomington, Illinois, Ray Smith of Mesquite, Texas, Karl von Mueller of Segundo, Colorado, and many other people have reported excellent success in this field. I also am pleased with the results of my underwater recovery work. Some have ingeniously devised portable rafts for floating their instrument as they scan the bottom with especially rigged search coils. One treasure hunter of Florida reported a great amount of recovered wealth. From the picture you can see the method he used to float his detector housing.

There is, of course, much more danger involved in this type of recovery than in a land search. Use all precautions. The bottom will be slippery. If you get out much above waist deep slight waves and undercurrents could easily pull you off your feet. If you use waders and were to fall, the waders would quickly fill with water which might lead to a very difficult situation. Always use extreme care and caution in any type of underwater salvage work.

LET A DREDGE DO THE WORK

As we already mentioned, probably half the valuables lost in a swimming area or around a swimming beach are lost in shallow water. This has been proved many times, not only by users of detectors with submersible search loops but, more recently, by persons using suction dredges. These are dredges primarily designed and built for prospectors and placer mining operations.

A suction dredge consists of a gasoline-driven engine

similar to your lawnmower engine, a water pump which is usually connected directly to the motor shaft, a suction hose, and nozzle. When the engine is driving the pump, suction is created at the end of the suction nozzle which causes not only water but also mud, rocks, coins, rings, fishing tackle — anything small enough to go through the nozzle opening — to be pulled up through the tube and deposited on a riffle board. A riffle board is a device similar to the old-time hand washboard, except that the riffle board is sometimes wider and several times longer. The purpose of the riffle board is to collect the heavier objects, such as gold nuggets, which are sucked up by the dredge. The heaviest objects fall into the troughs while the force of the water tumbles the lighter material on out the end of the board back into the water. Suction dredges are used in streams by prospectors to recover gold which has accumulated along the bottom of river beds in gold-bearing regions.

Suction dredges, when used along swimming beaches, will suck lost coins, rings, watches, and similar valuables up through the tube to be deposited either on the standard riffle board or into a wire mesh. My own dredge is equipped with a wire mesh basket. All objects pulled from the bottom are dumped into this mesh. Water, sand, and small objects fall through the mesh back into the water. Two people are needed in order to operate the dredge most efficiently, one person using the nozzle and the other, keeping the accumulated rocks, other debris, and, of course, the good finds — coins and rings — clear of the wire mesh to allow sand and water to pass through. Broken glass and fish hooks, among other things, will also be dumped into the basket. You are forewarned! Be prepared, especially for an occasional whole, live snake which will be pulled up through the dredge. If you are successful in locating and dredging some of the earlier swimming areas, of which there are thousands throughout the United States, you could quite easily pay for your entire dredge operation from just one of these clean-out operations.

Be very careful to keep the rubber tube or float balanced. The float must sit level in the water. If you mount the engine too far to one edge, the float will tip over or not float level. Also, be extra careful when operating an air inflated tube float because if the tube becomes punctured you can guess what happens.

WHAT SIZE DREDGE TO BUY?

Dredges are classified according to the diameter of the inside of the suction nozzle and hose. However, this is not the size of the nozzle opening. In order to create good suction and to prevent objects from entering the hose which are too large to pass through it, the opening of the nozzle is reduced and is always smaller than the diameter of the nozzle and hose. A two-and-a-half-inch suction dredge generally has an opening of two inches. A one-and-a-half-inch suction dredge has an opening slightly greater than one inch. You should consider these things when you are buying your dredge. Determine what is the largest sized object you want to retrieve from the bottom, and buy a dredge which has a rating of at least one-half-inch greater diameter. Of course, the larger the dredge, the greater the speed at which you can work. However, the larger the dredge, the heavier and more difficult it is to manage.

KARL VON MUELLER'S TIPS

Places where successful dredging for coins has been accomplished:

Arkansas River, Colorado — Underneath the bridge at Royal Gorge. Thousands of pennies and five-cent pieces have been recovered, as well as numerous rings and wristwatches. Coins found under the Royal Gorge bridge are usually thrown there as a good luck venture, and the jewelry that has been found is attributed to rings or watches falling off arms and fingers as a coin is flung.

Astoria Wishing Bridge — The site of the wishing bridge at the resort area of Astoria, Oregon, has been a good location. Metal detectors have been used along the banks and in the stream bed with some success. Gold coins recovered by dredging were often scarred and damaged.

Atlantic Coast Resort Areas—Numerous resort beaches and streams up and down the Atlantic coast have been worked with dredges with varying degrees of success. *Modus operandi* is usually to scout areas with a metal detector and, if enough coins are found to justify dredging and if dredging is feasible, a dredge is used.

Brown County, Indiana — Gold dredgers in streams in Southern Indiana occasionally find a small amount of coins, a retrieval that mystifies everybody as to how and why they got there.

Canadian River, New Mexico — For a quarter of a mile downstream from the Highway 85 bridge, hundreds of nickels and dimes have been found, mostly by treasure hunter Montana Larry Campbell and local residents. It is assumed this is loot from coin machine burglaries that was tossed over the bridge when pursuit was suspected by the thieves.

Padre Island, Texas — Suction dredgers attempted on several occasions to wash the beaches with suction dredges and similar devices. Randy Nufeld of San Diego, California, was probably the most successful by using a sluicebox device with a jet-tube to process huge amounts of beach sand.

Rosarita Beach, between Ensenada and Tiajuana, Baja California — Suction dredgers on the beach recovered hundreds of dollars in coin plus considerable jewelry until stopped by the Mexican authorities.

Russian River, near the town of Monte Rio, California — Thousands of coins have been recovered with dredges and metal detectors and nobody in town knows how they got there.

Southeastern U. S. — Numerous dredge operators work known locations along bayous in the southern states, mostly for relics, but they get some coin. Relics are sucked into the dredge nozzle and removed by hand. Most of the successful operators research the probable location of blockade-runners' loot and start working accordingly.

Suwanee River Boat Landing, below Old Town, Florida — Dredgers probed the old boat landing area and usually found coins and jewelry in pockets in the muck along the sides of the stream. All have quit due to the sedimentary and muddy nature of the stream bed.

GENERAL TIPS

Dredges should be operated at about 1/2 to 1/3 speed as coins are easily brought up. If there is too much pressure

Charles Garrett and Monty Moncrief of NASA, Houston, test several new land and submersible pulse and VLF trash elimination detectors. The salt water beach environment is one of the most demanding of search areas because of the moisture, the corrosive action of salt water, and the conductive nature of salt when wet (mineralization). Detectors must be well designed and manufactured in order to withstand beach operation. The particular units the men are operating are the new convertible water/land Sea Hunter XL500 instruments.

they are apt to be shot on through the riffle system and, because of their color, might not even be noticed in the water. A wire mesh system prevents loss, but can be slower because the mesh must be continuously cleaned of all debris. It is better to remove or bend the baffle in the sluicebox to deflect the coins to the top in order to avoid nicking or denting them. This is particularly important where gold coins are apt to be found. It is a good idea to put a screen across the sluicebox about half-way down to prevent coins being tumbled and washed on through. The usual screen is one-half-inch hardware screen. An extension pole can be attached to the nozzle to facilitate deep dredging. Never start a dredge without water in the pump. Always check out and test start your dredge before entering the deep water. It is frustrating to fool with a "crank" engine while standing in waist-deep water.

More and more husband and wife teams are taking up the sport of coin hunting, a hobby often rewarding as well as fun, since metal detectors can be used almost anywhere at any time to find coins, rings, and jewelry lost in recreational areas.

CHAPTER XI

Knowing, Finding and Keeping Track

Three important aspects of coin collecting as a hobby are *knowing, finding,* and *keeping track.* "Knowing" is the most interesting facet of coin collecting. "Finding" is the most thrilling; and "keeping track" so that you might "show" is the most satisfying.

KNOWING

How well do you know your coins? If today you were to dig up a 1970 clad, Denver half-dollar, in extra fine condition, what would you estimate as its worth according to Yeoman's "Red Book"? Fifty cents? One dollar? Fifteen dollars? If you guessed fifty cents, you get an "E" for effort. If you guessed fifteen dollars or more, go to the head of the class. This is just one example where "knowing" becomes one of the most interesting facets of coin collecting. Do you know what a braided hair half-cent or a "Hard Times" token is and their values? You make the hobby interesting and profitable by knowing the identity and value of coins, medallions, trade and tax tokens.

FINDING

After you have found several hundred "face value" coins the thrill of finding is generally diminished. But, do you recall your increased thrill and excitement when you found an old coin you knew was extra valuable? Thus, the thrill of finding is enhanced by knowing.

KEEPING TRACK

Lastly comes the most satisfying aspect, and that is in the keeping track and showing. Once you begin to see your coin albums and containers filling up you will begin to realize how satisfying this hobby can be.

SATISFYING AND REWARDING

The knowing, finding and keeping track aspects of coin collecting take on much greater importance when the coin collector is also a metal detecting coin hunter. How much more satisfying and rewarding it is to know that all the coins in your albums were found by your own sweat and toil. Don't neglect this perfect way to round out your coin-hunting activities. If you haven't begun to collect coins, to study them and know their values, then you should start

Charles and Vaughan Garrett and Frank Mellish of London, England, search this park in Holland. A trip through eight European countries was made in order to test the new Garrett ADS instrumentation being sold there. It was found that ground mineralization is an ever-present factor that requires the same or more exacting detector capabilities as are required in the United States. Coin hunting is truly fantastic wherever one travels in Europe. For countless centuries coins have been dropped and there has been hardly a detector in sight to find them! Frank Mellish is one of the most successful and best-known of British treasure hunters. Should your travels ever find you in London, be sure to go by his treasure hunting equipment shop, Treasure World, 155 Robert St., London, N.W. 1, England.

93

immediately. For $20 or so you can accumulate a small library of beginner's books, magazines, and coin containers. Several recommended books are listed in Appendix B.

HISTORY

People have been using coins since about 650 B.C. The first coins were struck in Asia Minor. These were bean-shaped lumps of gold, crudely stamped with a punch mark. Soon after, in Greece and Rome, coins flowered into things of beauty and fascinating historical interest. Since then, the people of the world have designed, made and distributed unknown trillions of coins, medallions, trade and tax tokens, and the like. Coin study is a world all its own, and a person could spend a lifetime studying and collecting coins and related items and still have scarcely even begun.

WHY COLLECT COINS?

People collect coins for many different reasons. Some, for the same reason that many people collect works of art

It's just as much fun checking dates and mint marks of coins discovered with a metal detector as it is to find them in the first place. Out-of-print U. S. Geological Survey maps of the type shown here proved useful in finding this day's take of old coins, some going back to 1865. An old hunting and prospectors' campground shown on this map as being along the Oregon Trail produced these coins . . . now the site is a modern forest camp alongside a busy U. S. Highway. Coins were found by Don Lien of Portland, Oregon. Photo courtesy Compass Electronic Corporation.

and masterpieces of painting and sculpture. Coins are miniature works of art, tiny sculptures by some of the world's
greatest artists set into durable metal. Each coin has a story
behind it . . . a tale of the triumphs and trials of a person, a
country, a philosophy, or a religion at some exciting and
crucial time in the history of mankind. Each coin has a
rich heritage and brings a wealth of pleasure and information to the collector.

There are many intriguing branches of numismatics
with which today's coin hunter will find himself suddenly
involved. Not only will you find coins, but you will find
trade tokens, commemorative medallions, military decora-
tions, tax tokens, convention badges, political campaign
buttons, foreign coins, and many other examples of man's
creativity in mediums of exchange.

TOKENS

While the United States was in the midst of the Great
Depression, the dollar shrank in value both at home and
abroad. Many of you will remember that 25% of the American work force was unemployed, and long bread lines appeared in most major cities. State and national governments
hovered on the edge of bankruptcy. As the national economic situation deteriorated, desperate state officials looked
for means of raising the revenues necessary for minimal
functioning. An income tax was out of the question; there
was simply not enough money circulating from salary pay-
ments to generate the money the states so desperately needed.
The ingenious solution arrived at by many states was a general levy of 2% on all retail purchases, thus, the sales tax. This
meant that for each item purchased for $1.00 the purchaser
was obligated to pay a tax of two cents to be turned over
to the state treasury as general revenue. To assure that the
state would receive the exact revenue due it the legislatures
of more than a dozen states authorized the creation of sales
tax tokens denominated in fractions of a cent. Today these
tokens serve as a unique reminder of the Great Depression
and one successful government effort to raise revenues in
the midst of it. As you search for coins you will find many
tax tokens. Some tax tokens were minted in quantities of
30,000,000 pieces, but even so these tokens have value today.
Aside from the monetary aspect, tax tokens are fun to collect, both in the sense that they are souvenirs of the Great
Depression and the years immediately following and that
they are among the last script issues of the various states.
With each tax token you find remember that you have just
recovered one of the last pieces of unique Americana
memorabilia of an era gone by.

Hardrock Hendricks and the Charles Garrett family sift in the dirt in search of Colorado Depression-days tax tokens. Some unknown person dumped more than 300 of these tokens here. The author discovered the site when he was walking along the fence in search of a ghost town location. The Garretts are using small hand-held sifters. Hardrock's one-man wire mesh sifter is propped against the fence.

WE FOUND SOMEONE'S COLORADO TAX TOKENS

During one trip to Colorado with my family I chanced to discover where someone had dumped several hundred Depression-day, two-cent Colorado tax tokens. I was walking along a fence row in search of a ghost town site when I spied one of the tokens lying on the ground. A kick in the dirt unearthed several more. I went to our vehicle to get my wife, Eleanor, and the children who returned to the location with me. We began sifting, and with each shovelful of dirt we found several more tokens.

A short time later Hardrock and Faye Hendricks drove along the road, spotted our vehicle, and walked down the fence row in search of us. (They had been spending the summer in Colorado, and Hardrock and I had just been searching for the ghost town.) They joined us in the sifting, and after an hour we concluded we had recovered all the tokens. The total find was more than three hundred! Most were stamped from metal; some were round and some were

All of these items were found by Glenn Carson in Mountain City, Colorado. The 1865 two-cent piece is in almost uncirculated condition. Glenn is the author of the popular book, COINSHOOTING, and compiler of THE TREASURE HUNTERS ANNUAL, which can be ordered from Carson Enterprises, Inc., 801 Juniper Avenue, Boulder, Colorado 80302.

Glenn Carson, Boulder, Colorado, found all of these items around old footings at Delagua, a coal camp south of Walsenburg, Colorado. The $1.00 trade token (upper right) is from Trinidad, a 10% trade discount advertising gimmick. Glenn stated that he has a $35.00 standing offer on a five-cent-drink bar token he found in nearby Tabasco. It was issued by the saloon keeper, C. G. Obrozzo.

97

square. A few were stamped from some type of red fiber or rubber. We are at a loss to explain why the tokens were there.

Another intriguing branch of numismatics is concerned with the extensive series of American tokens issued during the Civil War. They were about the size of our present-day penny, and were created in response to urgent demands by merchants for small change which had become very scarce. Tokens were either patriotic in theme or carried the name and address of the merchant, plus his own advertising message. Tokens offer us an intimate look at colorful slogans and patriotic sentiments, as well as the art work, of the Civil War period. Indians in feathered headdresses, liberty heads, Washington, Lincoln, Andrew Jackson, Stephen A. Douglas and Gen. George McClellan, appear on tokens, coupled with such intensely patriotic sentiments as, "The Union shall and must be saved," "The Flag of our Union. If anybody attempts to tear it down shoot him on the spot," and "No compromise with traitors." Others carry private interest group slogans, such as, "Millions for contractors; not one cent for the widows." Some merely stated, "Exchange for one cent" or "I owe you one cent."

FOREIGN COINS

You will be amazed at the number of foreign coins you will find. Frequently will you recover Canadian and Mexican coins. European coins are quite common also, perhaps because of the tremendous quantities brought back by soldiers of our two World Wars. These coins generally were given to children and, of course, lost. You may occasionally have the temporary thrill of finding a coin dated in the twelve or thirteen hundreds. The thrill ends abruptly when you discover the coin was dated using the Mohammedan calendar, not the Christian dating periods. Upon conversion the twelve or thirteen hundred date becomes one of the eighteen or nineteen hundreds.

MEDALLIONS

You will find interest in the commemorative medallions you will locate. Medallions date back to Roman times when they were issued to commemorate events of the day. Since then, medallions have been created in honor of famous people, events, animals, religion, and legends. Most medallions are beautiful works of art. They are being minted right up to the present to commemorate such subjects as animals, poets of the Western World, historic naval battles, presidents, military leaders, and entertainers. Try to learn the history behind each medallion you find. The knowledge will be rewarding. As for monetary worth, the greatest will be in the collectors' value.

CIRCULATIVE COINS

Your most important collections will be those United States Circulative Coins. You will be kept quite busy sorting and grading as you continuously add to and upgrade your coin albums. Inexpensive albums are available for most of the coin types that you will find. You will probably want to start with the most recently dated penny, nickel, dime and quarter albums. Your interest and enthusiasm in coin hunting will grow as you watch the albums fill. Coin collecting in itself will give you reason for wanting to get out on weekends to search for the older and better coin hunting spots. Keep your albums current. When you find a coin that is graded better than the coin already filling a slot in your album, place the more valuable coin in the album. Keep all loose coins grouped according to the same date and mint marks. Inexpensive plastic containers are available or, better yet, go to your bank and get free paper coin holders and write the identity of the coins on the outside.

INCREASES

In addition to the fact that coin collecting will add to your coin hunting interest, a well-thought-out collection will increase in value over the years and bring you substantially increased profits. One of the great joys of coin collecting has to be the possession of the knowledge that something you own or something that might come your way has real dollar value. While most of your coin finds will involve coins of nominal value, it is very definitely in the realm of possibility that you will occasionally discover a rare coin.

COIN DEALERS

Cultivate the friendship of other collectors or groups of coin hunters so that you can buy, sell, and swap coins. Most cities with a population of more than a few thousand have at least one coin dealer. He will be listed in the telephone directory Yellow Pages under the heading of "Coin Dealer" or perhaps "Stamps and Coin Dealers" or "Hobby Shops." Dealers generally are glad to appraise the value of a single coin at no charge, but it may be necessary to pay for the appraisal of a large accumulation. Coins may be sold to your local dealer or to dealers who advertise in hobby and coin publications. Always write to coin dealers before sending them your coins. They may have no interest in the particular coin or coins you have for sale. Most coin shops

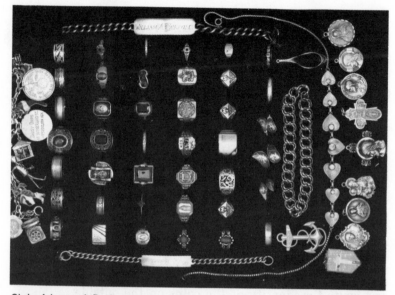

Chris Adams of Rochester, N. Y., found these rings, medallions, and jewelry items in parks and on swimming beaches.

This is just a few of the many thousands of coins and tokens found by Chris Adams of Rochester, N.Y. The original photograph is in color and brings out the beautiful brown, red, copper and silver colors that the coins acquire while buried.

have coin bid boards. You can place your coins, in plastic, see-through containers, on these boards for other buyers to inspect. The buyers, if interested, will bid on your coin. You can sell it to the highest bidder or just keep it. The fee for use of the bid board is generally some percentage of the amount you get for the coin.

HOW TO BEGIN

To begin your coin collecting hobby go to the library; read and study the books that interest you. Obtain the most recent Richard Yeoman Blue Guidebook and perhaps the Red one. For more current information try one or more of the weekly and monthly coin collecting papers and magazines. Drop a note to the American Numismatic Society Library, Broadway at 55th Street, New York City, for their list of recommended introductory books.

KNOW ITS VALUE

Don't ever sell or trade a coin without knowing its value. The Yeoman coin books are good guides, as are the weekly and monthly publications. The value of some coins is truly amazing. A 1909S VDB Lincoln cent in very good condition will pay for a metal detector. An 1873 Carson City quarter could be equivalent to a month's salary. Certain other coins could spell retirement.

To give you an idea of the value that some coins acquire I have chosen six coins recently sold or "bid" on the open bid market. It is not beyond the realm of possibility that the average coin hunter might recover one of these coins or any of many thousands that may not be quite as valuable but nevertheless could be sold for a great amount of money.

1907	Unique Indianhead double eagle ($20 gold coin)	$500,000
1855	Blake and Agnell $20 gold piece (See accompanying photo)	$300,000
1907	Saint Gauden's double eagle ($20 gold coin)	$150,000
1804	Silver dollar (Idler specimen)	$110,000
1913	Libertyhead nickel	$110,000
1794	Silver dollar	$110,000

The thrill that comes from finding just a plain, ordinary, everyday modern coin is great. Just think of the thrill that would come from recovering one of these five or any one, even, of their missing "kissing cousins." Keep after it. Just the thought of recovering valuable coins like these can keep you going full speed ahead.

Gene Rolls, Forest Ranch, California, displays only a few of the many coins and other relics he has found while searching mainly in old settlers' campgrounds and parks in Southern California. He can vividly relate the history behind every single one of his finds. Photo by Ray Rolls.

Estimates of $300,000 have been placed on the twenty-dollar gold piece being held by George Banks of Lewiston, Idaho. Only two similar coins are known to exist; one is owned by the Ford Foundation and the other is in the collection maintained by the Smithsonian Institution, according to Yeoman's coin manual.

Banks unearthed the valuable coin while using his Garrett metal detector on vacation in Washington State, August, 1974. He was searching the grounds of a long-deserted race track when the four years of using his metal detector to find coins for his collection really paid off. A resident in the area where Banks was vacationing mentioned the old race track, providing the clue which led the 61-year-old collector to his first gold coin.

The $20 gold piece is believed to have been minted during the last days of December, 1855, by Gorham Blake and a Mr. Agnell, owners of a gold smelter and assay office in Sacramento, California. The private minting of gold coin was sanctioned by the United States Government as early as 1848, in an effort to meet demands for more money in the rapidly growing California Territory. The letters S. M. V. engraved on the coin stand for "standard mint value," assuring that the coin met Federal standards in both weight and quality.

The exact worth of the coin will not be determined until it is sold, since rare coin value is usually determined by auction or highest bid. The two other California gold pieces are known to have sold for over $250,000, and an offer of $300,00 is believed to have been received. After the approximate value of the coin was learned, Banks immediately placed it in a bank vault where he says it will stay until a sale is made.

Mr. Banks is an electrician for the Potlatch Corporation in Lewiston, Idaho, and will retire in two years. His retirement security is now assured due to the proper use of his metal detector and his wise selection of a search site.

103

A coin authentication and evaluation service is now being offered by the International Numismatic Association, Authentication Bureau, P. O. Box 19386, Washington, D. C. 20036 (202-223-4496). It is recommended that anyone owning a coin he wishes to have examined and evaluated should give them a try. There is a fee for this service so be certain to contact them first with your inquiry. Be certain also to insure your coin adequately if you send it.

STOLEN COINS

I recently read an article of advice to coin collectors. The writer was advising the owners of coin collections to keep careful track of their coins, especially the more valuable ones, and the peculiarities of as many coins as possible. The writer stated that such descriptions could help identify a coin collection in the event it should be stolen. Write down the date, denomination and other numismatic characteristics of the coin, plus identifying features such as "scratch across the face," "nick on edge of the coin," "hole drilled in coin at top of coin," "diemark running through date," *etc.* This type of identification of your coins, kept in a safe place, could mean the difference between getting your coins back if they are ever stolen or not getting them back.

There are many things to consider if you want to get the most from your coin hunting and collecting hobbies. You will learn as you go along, but the knowing, finding and keeping track tie the two hobbies together. Don't delay —get started today!

CHAPTER XII

Rules and Laws for Coin Hunters

I believe the main rule we should remember when we find coins is "finders, keepers." If coins are lost — they are lost, period, and belong to the person who recovered them. Quite often, however, valuable rings and jewelry are lost. The person losing these items usually makes an honest, diligent effort to locate his lost treasure. Consider for a moment the thousands of lost class rings. (I am amazed how many are found.) Even though class rings have little monetary value the sentimental value is usually quite high. I have seen the happy faces of many people when they were suddenly presented with their old *alma mater* rings.

LOCATE OWNER

Always try to locate the owner of valuable jewelry you find. A class ring, of course, has the name of the high school, the graduation date, and in some cases, the initial of the person who owned it. I believe it will be more than worth your time to make an honest attempt to return these items to their rightful owners. Just the pride and satisfaction you will receive from returning a lost article will make the day go better. Often, too, generous rewards are given to the finders of valuable jewelry, and even more often the resulting "finder's publicity" you will receive in the newspaper and by word of mouth can lead to other valuable leads and areas to search. Stories of this type printed in newspapers will prompt many people to ask you to help in their search for lost articles or for Grandpa's gold. People are willing to pay up to half the value to recover items they have lost. Honesty and a respect for the property of others govern the coin hunter.

LAWS

Laws on most city dockets prohibit anyone from destroying public or private property. When you dig a hole or cut through the grass on private or public property, you are, in effect, violating a law. However, these laws generally are not enforced, especially if the coin hunter is careful in his retrieving. An experienced coin hunter (and treasure hunter) will thoroughly search an area, retrieve all valuable items, and leave without anyone knowing he or she was there. On the other hand, thoughtless and sometimes inexperienced treasure hunters can completely devastate a given treasure site, leaving large gaping holes, tearing down buildings, and tearing up sidewalks. I have seen much destruction by a few people. Damage of this kind is one of the reasons why recently-enacted laws were designed to shut down and restrict the treasure hunter. There have always been laws to protect public lands, but only during the past few years have these laws been enforced by local governmental enforcement agencies. It is quite easy to understand, however, why this has happened. Public lands, parks, recreational areas, are continuously maintained and kept in good condition so those using them will enjoy them to the fullest. When there is willful destruction, laws are enacted or existing laws are enforced. Chapter IX discusses various methods you can use to retrieve coins and other objects without destroying the grass and making unsightly messes.

REFILL THOSE HOLES!

Of increasing concern is the criticism and even outlawing of the use of metal detectors in public places. It is high time that all detector owners and treasure hunting hobbyists realize that they should work toward a common goal and definite ideals. No other sport or hobby has been so totally dedicated to delving into history and recovering objects of both intrinsic and nostalgic value. Yet, in the general field of exploration so many coin and treasure hunters have overstepped their bounds . . . and too often not just a little!

A recent article in an Eastern newspaper stated that a city ordinance will be added to a town's school code to stop coin hunting on schoolgrounds and public beaches and parks. Anyone " . . . out for underground booty could be smacked with a fine of $500, plus charges of criminal damage to property and trespass." How does that strike you! The article stated that since coin searching began the city parks and property owned by the schools, including the football field, have become pock-marked with the digs of money hunters, ruining sod and creating conditions which could cause players to twist an ankle easily. The article further noted that football players run enough risks without having to dodge holes left by treasure hunters. Holes had also been dug in the baseball diamonds. "If we let it go on, our property will be a mess," it was stated. This is typical of what is happening in too many cities.

A few words to the wise: let's make that extra effort to improve our image; let's improve our manners and refill and level spots where we've dug any kind of hole (whether for a pot or a penny); let's show that treasure hunting enthusiasts are just as interested in preservation as they are in exploration and discovery! In the past metal detectors sounded on coins to about six inch depths, but now, with the new VLF type instruments which give much deeper penetration, all manufacturers are really urging you . . . treasure hunters, FILL THOSE HOLES!

PAY UNCLE?

The United States Income Tax laws are very definite in regard to the income tax a person must pay on all his income. Any treasure you find must be treated as income. However, you pay income tax only in the year in which you sell the items for cash or in the year in which you placed your newly-found coins back in circulation. If you find valuable artifacts and keep them, you do not pay taxes until these items are sold. When you sell the items, the amount you get should be considered income in that year.

It stands to reason that in any activity in which there is income that must be reported, then by all rights any expenses incurred in the recovery or acquisition of this income must be deductible. Keep accurate records of all expenses involved in coin hunting and treasure hunting. Keep track of your mileage, all purchases such as detector batteries, maps, shovels, compasses, tools, and so on, and deduct these expenses the year in which you incur them or in the year you sell some of your "finds."

CHAPTER XIII

Cleaning Your Coins

TO CLEAN OR NOT TO CLEAN

In most cases it is advisable to make no attempt to clean coins, other than just a general light soaking in mild soapy water (do not use dishwasher detergent; use only liquid soap). The slightest damage to a coin can degrade its numismatic value. Coin collectors prefer to buy coins as they are found and do their own cleaning rather than have someone attempt to clean a coin and destroy its value. If you *must* clean your coins there are several methods you may try.

ELECTROLYSIS

One is the use of electrolysis. There are several electrolysis cleaners on the market, and one works as good as another. These cleaners work on the principle of the removal of a tiny portion of the coin's surface by sending a small current through the coin while it is submerged in a solution of water and citric acid. Generally, a small one-cup-size glass is used with a stainless steel electrode about the size of a tongue-depressor, submerged into the water. One terminal of a low voltage (3 to 6 volts) supply is applied to this stainless steel electrode. The circuit is then completed when the other terminal is attached to the coin by means of an alligator clip or some kind of spring tension device. A direct current of ten mils to 100 mils is generally passed through the coin. The higher the current, the faster the surface metal will be removed from the coin. The metal, as it is removed from the coin, breaks up the surface corrosion. Coins are usually left in the bath from one to about ten minutes. Following the electrolysis bath the coins must be scrubbed with a small, soft brush.

On some coins this technique works quite well; however, it is easy to damage your coin permanently unless great care is taken in keeping the liquid either clean or separated for the different types of coins. Nickels should be cleaned in their own bath, pennies in their own bath, and silver coins in their own bath. Otherwise, nickels when cleaned in a penny solution will turn red, and so on. The multi-metal clad coins now in circulation can create similar problems. Coin cleaners of the electrolysis type are generally used on very badly corroded coins such as those which have been submerged in salt water for long periods of time.

108

LIQUID CLEANERS

I have tried many different types of liquid or immersion cleaning, achieving varying degrees of success. I have tried the following cleaning agents or commercial cleaning liquids: Tarn-X, olive oil, Rings and Things, Bulova Liquid Jewelry Cleaner, Twinkle, NIC-A-LENE, a paste of baking soda and water, an ammonia solution, and a solution of salt and white vinegar. The two most effective commercial cleaners are Twinkle and NIC-A-LENE. These two cleaners do a reasonably good job; however, they are expensive and they do have a peculiar odor. My favorite cleaning liquids are olive oil and the solution of white vinegar and salt. Surface corrosion on coins soaked in olive oil anywhere from an hour to several days will be loosened sufficiently so that a small brush will complete the cleaning process. The solution of salt and vinegar does the best and quickest job, but a little more care is required to use it. The best cleaning brush I have found is called NIC-A-BRUSH. It is a small, fine wire brush that can be used to clean stubborn corrosion from coins; however, let me warn you . . . it does cause some amount of surface damage, in proportion to the pressure you use and the length of time you rub with the brush.

If I were to recommend a cleaning method it would be using the white vinegar and salt solution, followed by a very light brushing, if necessary. Then, to protect your coin, wrap it in aluminum foil or place in a tarnish-proof coin envelope.

Before getting into this cleaning method in detail, let me give you some words of caution. If you find jewelry which has a cheap, paste stones, leave it alone except perhaps for a very mild soaking in a soapy solution. Use extreme caution in cleaning jewelry that has mounted pearls, opals, turquoise, and coral.

WHITE VINEGAR AND SALT

Bob Grant, Editor of TREASURE SEARCH magazine, printed the following article on coin cleaning in TREASURE SEARCH. It is surely an excellent method to clean coins and will save us all a lot of time.

"Anyone who has spent any time coinshooting knows what it is to sit down and try to clean the tarnish off a day's find in small change! And none of us wants to carry a sack of dirty coins into a bank and ask the teller to exchange it for crisp new bills.

"If coinshooting is your hobby and you do it often you know that most commercial coin cleaners can be expensive and carry warnings about getting any of it on your skin or inhaling its vapors. With the coinshooter's problem in mind, I offter this aid. My system is inexpensive and harmless, as well as time saving.

"Equipment Needed:
    2 small drinking glasses
    1 rinse can (one pound coffee cans are excellent)
    Table salt
    White vinegar

The reason for two glasses is that separate solutions are used for copper and silver coins. Using the same solution for both often turns your silver coins pink or copper colored.

"Step 1: The Solution To make the solution pour one teaspoonful of table salt into a glass. Add one ounce of white vinegar.

"Be sure to make two solutions if you will be cleaning both copper and silver coins. The above solution will clean about six to eight coins at a time. You may double contents for quicker results and to clean more coins at a time, but the solution you now have is working fast and some coins will be ready to take out in just seconds. Do not attempt more at a time than you can watch, or the coins will turn dull if left too long in the solution. Of course if they do stay too long the dullness will not harm the monetary value, and the dullness will not look as unsightly as the tarnish, but the best job is done when the coins get rinsed in time.

"Step 2: The Rinse For this part have your rinse can full of cold water and left under a slow running tap. As the coins show brightly in the solution remove them and drop them in the rinse. Some coins will be stubborn and not want to come clean, but you can help them along by removing them and rubbing with your fingers, then dropping them back into the mix. Few coins may need to stay in the mix for an hour, but most will come clean in seconds or minutes. After the coins are rinsed for about three minutes you can wipe them, or spread them out on a paper towel to dry.

"This method I have described is for coins that are tarnished. Those badly encrusted coins that won't come clean in the solution will have to be scrubbed with steel wool, or whatever other system you may prefer, then dropped back into the solution. Those will be few and your scrubbing is far less than before you used this method.

"You will want to keep in mind that this method is only recommended for coins that are to be put back into circulation. Collectible and valuable coins should never be cleaned except by experts.

"Just a little experimenting with the salt and vinegar and you can learn to hasten or slow down the cleaning process to your own satisfaction."

The Rev. John Costas, 116 W. Lincoln Way, Wheatland, IA 52777, has been hunting coins for several years. He uses a VLF/TR Deepseeker to find the deep coins in this yard. The Rev. Costas has found many thousands of coins and dozens of diamond rings, all of which help to maintain a college fund for his children.

WHEN TO CLEAN COINS

During your search for and recovery of coins it is advisable not to clean them as soon as they are recovered. Two main reasons are: (1) in trying to rub or clean the dirt off the coin there is a possibility you may scratch or mar the surface; (2) it takes time away from your coin hunting. Just consider the time spent attempting to clean coins while you are hunting. You'll see you could perhaps double your take if you just place them in your "goodies" bag and go on with your coin hunting. Later, when you get home, put the coins gently in a wooden or plastic bowl of a mild soapy solution. Do not use dishwasher powders or harsh kitchen detergents. Do not let the coins lie one on top of another. After they have soaked a few minutes a very light rubbing will remove most dirt and contamination and let you behold the beauty of your coins. If you want to clean them better you can use any one or a combination of the cleaning methods already described in this chapter.

AGED LOOK IS BEAUTIFUL

Keep in mind, however, it is advisable not to clean the coins beyond the detergent soaking and light rubbing. If you talk with coin dealers you will find, I think, unanimous agreement that they would rather buy coins that have not been cleaned, except perhaps of loose surface contamination. They say they prefer coins with the natural, aged look and, also, if you do happen to come across an extremely valuable coin you could greatly reduce its value by improper cleaning. To me, coins that retain the normal colors after they have in the ground for certain periods of time are far more beautiful than coins that have been made shiny or perhaps streaked by poor cleaning attempts.

PRESERVE IRON RELICS

Frequently the coin hunter will dig up valuable iron relics. If the relics have been buried for many years or if they have been buried in highly-mineralized soil, such as that type of soil found on the beach, the object could be fairly well rusted. When it is retrieved from the ground and cleaned off, exposing it to the air, it can continue to deteriorate at a rapid rate. If you wish to preserve an iron object, paint it with a coating of polyurethane varnish. The varnish will stop air from reaching the surface and prevent further rusting or deterioration.

COIN CLEANER

Write to Ernie Curlee's Treasurehouse, 3201 Cullman Avenue, P.O. Box 26632, Charlotte, NC 28213. Tell him you want information on his new coin cleaning machine. It is a very good, efficient cleaner and the cost is low.

CHAPTER XIV

"Odds and Ends" of Successful Coin Hunting

When writing a book such as this one, there are always a few "odds and ends" that just don't seem to fit in anywhere. Thus, I have set aside this chapter for those discussions that do not seem to fit in anywhere else.

MANY CALL IT "COINSHOOTING"

Many detector operators and coin hunters are familiar with the term "coinshooting." The term was coined by Karl von Mueller many years ago, but whether it be called "coin hunting" or "coinshooting," it's great fun.

TWO QUESTIONS

One question I have been asked perhaps more than any other is how deeply will a detector find coins. Perhaps the second most frequently-asked question is why coins become covered. The answers to these two questions are somewhat complex.

Coins that drop to the ground can either become buried more deeply or they can stay basically right on the surface. Many things determine whether a coin will be buried and, if so, how deeply . . . the amount of sand and dirt that blows in that area, the quantity of rainfall, the amount of foot traffic by people or animals, erosion, meteorite fallout, dust storms, and even the normal, natural settling due to the weight of the coin. Fortunately, most coins that are lost and buried are lying flat in the ground. Since metal detectors are surface area detectors, the detector will produce a greater signal if the coin is lying flat than if it is standing on edge. Test this for yourself with any detector. Turn on the instrument, tune it in the metal mode according to manufacturer's instructions, and slowly bring a coin up toward the bottom side of the search coil. You will notice the signal beginning to increase to a loud pitch as you come close to the bottom of the search coil. Rotate the coin ninety degrees so that the coin is no longer "looking" at the bottom of the search coil. You will notice a sudden decrease in the magnitude of the signal. This proves that the greater the metal surface area that is "looking" at the search coil, the greater the signal. As we said, detectors are surface area detectors.

Luckily, when most coins are lost they fall to the ground and do lie flat. As they become covered they generally stay in this flat position. . . a happy circumstance for all of us coin hunters since a coin lying flat can, as we have seen, be detected at a greater depth than a coin standing on edge. Also, the larger the physical size of a coin, the more deeply it can be detected. Many factors influence how deeply a coin or any metallic object can be detected: the size and shape of the object; the type of ground; how long the object has been buried; how it is lying in the ground; ground moisture content; detector quality; and the skill of the operator. You will learn all about these factors as you coin hunt. The more you learn about your detector, ground problems, and buried target responses, the more proficient and successful you will become.

TOOLS

The second-most important accessory in coin hunting (your detector is first) is your digging tool. (See also Chapter IX.) Depending upon the area you are searching and the type of ground you encounter, your tools will include one or more of these: a screwdriver; a probe; a knife; a small garden hand rake; a trowel; a sifter; some other type of leverage tool; a leaf and trash rake; and a weed cutter. If in coin hunting you encounter different types of soil, you may need more than one of the above-mentioned tools. Study the chapter entitled HOW TO DIG THAT COIN! before selecting your recovery tools.

In addition you will need a small bag suspended from your belt or a coin hunting apron with at least two pockets, made either of waterproof plastic or with plastic pocket liners. Quite often you will be digging in areas that are wet. When you retrieve coins from the ground, especially muddy ground, some of the soil will stay with the coin until you have had an opportunity to clean it. This accumulation of damp soil can cause the contents of non-waterproofed pockets to leak through onto your clothing. Determine in which pocket you will be placing valuable finds and into which one you will be placing the trash (bottle caps, nails, foil, and so on). Recover and properly dispose of all junk you find because it is likely you will return to the same spot to search again, or another coin hunter will try his luck there. Even if you do not return, the absence of metal in the ground will alert future coin hunters that the ground has already been searched. In addition, park caretakers will love you because you are helping keep the area clean. Often, when these persons learn what you are doing and realize that you are actually helping them keep the park clean they will give you valuable information you can use for more successful searching. They may be able to tell you where people have congregated and, consequently, where coins are most likely to be found. They can tell you the former location of picnic tables, playground equipment, and other centers of activity that might help you locate "hot spots."

Always carry a pen and pencil with you to make notes of your finds and ideas that come to mind as you coin hunt. In coin hunting, like anything else, you learn by doing. As you coin hunt you will discover your mistakes, and you will develop your own particular recovery style and new and better ways to coin hunt.

Here's a good tip from "Pinky" Nobel, Lewiston, Idaho. He gives instructions on how to build a coin probe. Cut a piece of 3/32-inch piano wire approximately twelve inches long. Cut a 4½-inch length of broom handle and drill a 3/32-inch hole down the center of this handle four inches deep. Force the piano wire into the hole all the way to the bottom. Round off the end of the wire until it is smooth. Then . . . probe carefully!

HOORAY FOR SENATOR JOHN McCUME!

This bit of interesting news was recently printed in the Indian Territory Treasure Hunters Club news bulletin. "Sen. John McCume, Rep., Oklahoma City, recently introduced legislation to outlaw the sale of so-called 'pop top' cans. Environmentalists and wildlife enthusiasts (and TH'ers, too!) dislike the cans. The millions of pulltabs that are carelessly thrown upon the ground each year clutter the countryside and are responsible for the death of thousands of fish each year. McCume's proposal states that anyone who shall sell or offer for sale at retail in this state (Oklahoma) any metal beverage container designed and constructed so that a part of the container is detachable without the aid of a can opener shall be guilty of a misdemeanor."

Hooray for Sen. McCume! How great it would be if metal detector operators did not have to contend with pulltabs. This is another reason why detector operators should keep all found pulltabs and discard them in the trash. Soon, perhaps, if all pulltop cans are outlawed, the pulltop plague may be eliminated.

WHAT'S YOUR PERCENTAGE?

In most cases when you are searching with others, the coins you find are yours. If you are searching on another man's property, one-half the face value of a good recovery should be yours. When you wish to search another man's property, it is best always to have a prior agreement, either verbal or written. It is better to take home half of something than "nothing of something."

WHEN TO COINHUNT?

Anytime you want to! Day or night, morning or evening. Rain, shine, sleet, or snow — all seasons are coin hunting seasons. As I already pointed out, perhaps the greatest benefit to be derived from coin hunting is the health benefit. You will soon learn that coin hunting requires much effort, but you will also learn it is worth it. You will increase your stamina and endurance, and you should become much more healthy as a result of your coin hunting endeavors. After your evening meal you might go to a local park or swimming pool and search for an hour or so. On weekends you can spend up to full-time in searching outlying and out-of-town sites. On vacations make it a habit to stop along the roadway at the various parks; stretch your legs, refresh yourself and your family, and also search and recover a few goodies which have been lost by persons who stopped just ahead of you. It's a good way to limber up in the morning and get the blood circulating. Get up an hour earlier; drive to the park or into the downtown area and search along heavily congested traffic areas. Get out before most people do; the rewards will be yours. If you work in an area close to a park or any location where people play or congregate, during lunch break walk over and coin hunt. Anytime you are driving along and see an area that looks promising — stop, get out with your detector and try. You never know what you may uncover.

CRISS-CROSS

If you are confronted with a large area and you are not sure if that area will be productive or contain coins, it is best to criss-cross the area with a few well-planned passes. One method is to make a complete pass across one side of the area. Then move over a few feet, say ten feet, and make a second pass parallel to the first pass. Make notes when you find coins. Then go back and work in the spots where you first found coins. Never make an attempt to begin scanning in any given area until you have done all you can to determine where the "hot spots" are.

YOU SHOULD COMPLETELY COVER A GOOD AREA

There are several techniques which coin and treasure hunters utilize to make certain they have accurately and completely covered the area they are searching. A large

116

This Memphis, Tennessee, waterfront cobblestone area was laid more than 100 years ago. It is likely that thousands of valuable coins lie in the cracks and crevices between the rocks. There will be lots of coins standing on edge . . . so go prepared to hear many faint signals.

The author holds a two-ounce silver nugget he found in the boardwalk area that paralleled the main street of Altman, Colorado. Altman was a prosperous mining town back in the late 1800's and early 1900's. The nugget is kept in the Garrett Gold Collection which contains hundreds of gold and silver nuggets (some as large as seven pounds) found all over the world by treasure hunters using the new VLF/TR metal/mineral detectors.

area can be blocked off mentally into given smaller areas. The small areas can be searched, one at a time, until the entire area has been covered. In places where there are trees, benches, and other markers, it is easy for the operator to cover the ground completely without any skipping. However, in open areas, such as fields and large parks, it is difficult without some kind of markers to know for certain that an area has been completely searched.

Some persons drive small stakes into the ground and tie a string between the stakes. (Golf tees make good markers and can be used for other things besides. See Chapter XVII.) They make their first pass along the length of the string with either the right or left end of the detector search coil sweep touching this line. When they have scanned the full string length, they move their string over the width of the search coil swing and repeat the same process. Some people utilize only markers which they push into the ground and do not use the string. This method is probably satisfactory, at least for short distances. The more experience you have the better you will be able to search a given area completely without the use of markers or string.

But — cover the entire area you must! Do not get in a hurry. The coin which you are looking for and hurrying to find on the other side of the park may be right at your feet. Take your time and do a thorough job.

PINPOINTING TROUBLES?

One thing all coin hunters must learn to do is to pinpoint detected coins accurately. Accurate pinpointing not only speeds up recovery, but it reduces damage done to the digging area. If you have trouble pinpointing try these two methods. (See also Chapter IX.) After you have first detected your target continue passing over the spot while rotating the tuning control so that the instrument tuning backs down into the null or quiet zone. As you do this you will note your detector indication becoming more narrow until you have reached the tuning point where the detector is giving only a sharp and perhaps weak audio "blip." Your coin will be directly beneath the place on your coil where the loudest signal over detected metal objects normally occurs.

The second method is to begin raising your coil slightly higher in the air each time you pass over the detected object. The signals will get weaker and weaker until you finally hear only a faint "blip" or audio increase. Again, the metal object will be directly beneath your coil's known maximum signal area. This second method is generally a little more difficult because your coil will be airborne, and it will be somewhat more difficult to locate the exact spot on the ground.

KEEP RECORDS AND SCORE

From the start get into the habit of logging in your daily finds. You should keep track not only of the good stuff but also the junk you recover. Regardless of the type instrument you use, the more you use it the more proficient you will become, and the ratio of "good" to "bad" targets recovered will become greater and greater in favor of the "good" things. The better you understand your detector's signals, the more junk (bottle caps, foil, *etc.*) you will leave in the ground. Thus, a daily record is valuable for it will show your progress and allow you to keep score as you watch accumulations of coins and other goodies grow day by day.

SPECIALIZE

Perhaps, in addition to your general coin hunting, you should specialize in searching certain areas like fairgrounds, parks, old circus grounds, ghost towns, old church grounds, *etc.*

JERRY NUNN

The following is a capsule of an article printed in in TREASURE SEARCH magazine.

"Jerry Nunn of Charlotte, N.C., an accomplished weekend coin hunter, is interested only in *old* coins, and he specializes in church yards (not graveyards), established in the last century or earlier. In a period of less than three years he has taken more than 2,000 coins out of old church-yards in Maryland and North Carolina. Of these 2,000 coins, 500 of them are rare enough to be worth more than face value. The oldest is an 1822 large cent piece, and the most valuable is a 1901-O Barber quarter worth about $70. His largest haul consisted of 100 coins that he found in the yard of a one-room church outside Washington, D. C. Jerry states that church yards are the best places because you don't have to worry about weeds, and usually you can get permission especially after they see you are not going to spade up the yard and leave holes. Also, churches are quite accessible."

JIM WATSON

Jim Watson of Greenville, Texas, specializes in searching old settlers' campgrounds. From one such campground located near Sherman, Texas, Jim retrieved more than 2,000 old coins, dated between 1875 and 1925. "I still cannot believe the quantity of coins I retrieved from that campground," Jim reports. He further states, "There is one thing about coin hunting in these old places, and that is that most of the coins will be old because very few of the old campgrounds I have found are in use today."

BOB BARNES' GOOD SUGGESTION

Bob Barnes, father of the yearly Oklahoma City Shepherd Mall TH-ers show, recommends that city park hunters search the grassy areas adjacent to the sidewalks and streets. From experience he has found that often these areas are "fantastic" while the playground areas are worked to death.

IF YOU DO

If you have a desire to specialize in certain coin hunting areas and locations there is one simple way to choose the type of area in which you wish to specialize. Continue coin hunting in different areas as you do now. The first time you find an area that is extremely "hot" and contains many old valuable coins, choose that particular type of coin hunting site as your specialty. Some suggestions, in addition to those mentioned above, are old and unused drive-in theaters, sites of old country and general stores, areas where fire or flood have wiped out communities, natural water springs, plus dozens of other places too numerous to mention.

DON'T BE "BUGGED"

Every year people who venture into the out-of-doors are stung or bitten by spiders, ticks, hornets, scorpions, bees, wasps, ants, and the like. Usually pain, sickness, soreness, sometimes even death, result. The greatest danger from most of these attacks is during the spring and summer. There is very little danger during cold weather. To avoid being stung by wasps, bees, or other flying insects, you should not use scented preparations such as deodorants, hair spray, and perfume. Keep an aerosol insecticide spray with you in case of need. If you are allergic to these stings, consult your doctor as to the type of medication and treatment you need in the event of a sting. It is a good idea to make a trip to see your doctor or to the drugstore to get good medication or advice on how to treat stings BEFORE you venture out! You are most likely to be bitten by spiders around old buildings, old lumber, city dumps, and trashy areas or areas which have not been disturbed in some time. Scorpions are common especially in the Southern states. To prevent spider, scorpion and similar bites watch where you put your hands and feet. Wear heavy work gloves when moving debris and lumber. Look on the underside of lumber *before* picking it up, if possible. If you can, use a good pesticide in these areas before working them. It is advisable to stay out from under old buildings, porches, and so on, unless you proceed cautiously and carefully inspect the area before doing so. Ticks give us all fits. Their season starts in March and ends in August, with the peak in May, June and July.

ON-LOOKERS

You must accept the fact that when you coin hunt, especially on public property, you will be asked questions. It is best that you tell the inquisitive person you are coin hunting or searching for coins which have been lost. If you give a man an answer to his question then he should in return give you an answer to yours. Why don't you ask him if he knows of any good places you might locate coins? If you briefly explain to him what coin hunting is all about he may reward you with several fruitful locations. If the police quiz you tell them what you are doing. Rarely will they bother you further or cause you any discomfort, especially if you have been careful about covering all of your holes, and if you show them all the junk you have collected which you are about to throw in the trashcan.

Most policemen know what metal detectors are because they use them in their weapons recovery work. And, too, you might as well get it over with. If the policeman goes away and leaves you alone, then in all probability you can search the rest of the parks in your town without being bothered again. If he asks you to leave, go quietly and quickly and thank the officer for his courtesy. As an added thought, you might explain to the officer what you know about metal detectors and their capabilities. In the event this local police department has not utilized a detector for weapons search and for an occasional investigation, offer, if you wish, your services. Tell him you would be glad to help in a search in the event they ever need to locate lost or hidden metallic objects. I know of at least one-half-dozen cases in Dallas alone where metal detectors during the past year have been quite helpful to the police department. A quarter-million-dollar stolen jewelry cache was recovered by a detector. The same instrument also recovered the ejected cartridge of a bullet that killed a public official. The discovery of this cartridge led to the capture and conviction of the guilty party. A similar detector which was equipped with an underwater coil located a downed, submerged helicopter.

There are many questions you will be asked by on-

121

lookers, and within a short time you will have learned the correct answers to give.

DO IT AGAIN!

Throughout any day of normal coin hunting your detector will emit many signals, and consequently you will dig many holes. Often, when a coin hunter digs up a valuable coin he becomes quite excited. I want to bring to mind here a thought. When you retrieve any metallic object from a hole, always scan over the hole in order to determine if additional metal objects are still buried. There are many cases where more than one coin or more than one metal object has been retrieved from the same hole.

BUSINESS CARDS

Since the IRS looks upon your profitable hobby as a business, why don't you? Have a few hundred inexpensive cards printed. Only one good lead from all these cards which you can hand out to people you meet while coin hunting can pay for the cards many times over. Keep the cards simple. They might say something like, "Have metal detector. I'll help you find your lost valuables . . . coins, rings, jewelry are my specialty!" Then give your name, address and/or telephone number. You can give quantities of these to your local jeweler, insurance agent, people in sporting goods shops, hobby shops, place them on bulletin boards in drug stores, laundromats, supermarkets, and like places.

PATIENCE! PATIENCE!

As Abe Lincoln said (Mr. L. L. Lincoln, an active coin and treasure hunter), "One of the prime requisites of successful coin hunting is patience." You *must* learn to develop patience! Granted, you should develop a fast scanning technique, but you should never be in such a hurry to scan an area that you may pass over coins which are buried directly in front of you. Also, many persons become impatient because they do not find coins, or, if they do find them, the coins may have little or no more than face value. Here again, much patience is required. Let me assure you that there is a vast quantity of wealth waiting beneath your feet, and you can locate this wealth if you will simply learn to master your instrument, use your head in selecting the areas where you will search, be patient, and take your time to cover all areas thoroughly.

BACKACHES! BACKACHES!

Yes! You will have them more often than not; however, this is one of the best exercises for strengthening the

The author digs coins along the front street walk areas in a ghost town near Anaconda, Colorado. Many ghost town property owners allow minor digging for coins and artifacts, but when destruction of the buildings, however slight, occurs, then all visitors are considered trespassers and rightly so.

muscles of the entire back area, as well as those of the arms and legs. If you are the typical moderate-to-fast-scanning coin hunter you will operate slightly bent over. If you remain in this position for long periods you will find it difficult to straighten up. Thus, make it a habit every few minutes to stop, straighten up, rest a moment, then go again. A slight hand massage of the small part of the back will greatly relieve fatigue and aching muscles. Also, it helps to take a short walk or do a few toe touches. Let me give you some encouragement, however. After a few days of searching with your instrument, muscle ache will disappear, and you will think nothing of searching six or eight hours a day. Whatever soreness and stiffness you experience, the physical rewards will make it all worthwhile.

OTHER AREAS OF INTEREST

There is one thing most coin hunters learn rapidly. Their metal detecting activities quickly lead them into other areas of interest. Good research is a prime requisite in locating good places to coin hunt. Thus, you may become a historian in your own right rather soon. As you do your research don't fail to look for other things of value which may be awaiting your discovery. All forms of treasure hunting should be seriously considered as you go about your coin hunting.

Other major areas of interest in treasure hunting are nugget shooting, prospecting, cache hunting, bottle hunting, and relic hunting. These are all popular THing activities and should become a regular part of your program. On vacations as you travel around to the various coin hunting areas keep your eyes open and be alert to other possibilities as they come along. Suggested readings . . . in reality, "musts" . . . are books like Karl von Mueller's THE TREASURE HUNTER'S MANUALS #6 and #7, Roy Lagal's "HOW TO TEST" DETECTOR FIELD GUIDE, and several others listed in the back.

Expand your horizons; increase your interests and activity into things around you. Treasure hunters quite frequently become experts in Indian lore. Indians lived and roamed everywhere. One of my side hobbies which developed as a result of my treasure hunting interests is Indian lore. I have surveyed the Comanche war trail which leads from Kansas down through Oklahoma, New Mexico and Texas. I have located several Indian encampments, many artifacts, arrowheads and implements. I discovered the burial sites of two Indian chiefs, one I named "Chief Stone Mountain," and I discovered the location of a three-acre Indian burial ground. I directed the local archaeologists to these sites.

If you are interested only in coin hunting, that's up to you. But, at least the other activities are there, and what does it hurt to strengthen your knowledge about them?

CHAPTER XV

Tips from SUCCESSFUL COIN HUNTING Readers

Many readers have written to me since SUCCESSFUL COIN HUNTING was first published in 1974. A number of their tips and suggestions have been included within this revision, especially in this chapter. I am indebted to these people for taking the time to write and to share their ideas and experiences with others. I have given credit whenever it was possible to do so. Since I plan to revise SUCCESSFUL COIN HUNTING approximately every two years in order to bring the coin hunting and metal detector sections up to date, I invite all of you to write to me. Let me know what you would like to see included in the next revision.

NEW PLACES TO SEARCH

Mr. J. B. Estes (see page 63) sent in these good tips. Always scan the backbone of books with your detector. He does this at all flea markets and garage sales he attends. He says many people hide coins in the backbone of hardcover books. (Look on the backbone of SUCCESSFUL COIN HUNTING — you will see an Indianhead penny, a five-dollar gold piece and a Liberty dime!) J. B. said he has found several coins this way, among which were TWO GOLD COINS! J. B. also suggests you search around fireplaces. He reports he has found coins hidden between fireplace bricks. He thinks children must have hidden them there and then forgotten they did so.

Mr. and Mrs. Harry Bowen submitted the following as good places around which to search: baptismal areas; faucets in parks; bases of old trees (oldtimers would throw their coats here when they worked nearby and coins and other things fell from pockets); Prohibition-time "Whisky Rocks." A "Whisky Rock" is a designated place (a rock, maybe a tree stump, *etc.*) where a whisky peddler would leave his beverages. Someone would retrieve the whisky, leaving money in its place. As far back as the early 1800's this practice was common around construction gangs where the sale of whisky was not permitted on the job. As a last suggestion from the Bowens, check with your city engineer's office to locate places which are to be or have been demolished. As written in other places in SUCCESSFUL

COIN HUNTING, all condemned areas make good coin and treasure hunting sites!

Here is a tip from my files for which I have no name to credit: always check vending machine and telephone coin slots. About one out of every three or four times you will find coins others have left behind.

Dick Ferrick sent in another good tip. He said he has been successful in finding coins and other pocket things under and around telephone and light poles and guy wires. Apparently, he says, kids play around those places; he knows for certain they lose things!

This suggestion comes from W. G. Eslick. He strongly encourages coin hunters to search and re-search all known coin producing areas. He said that with meticulous searching anyone will probably find coins in areas that have been worked many times before. This suggestion of Mr. Eslick's is very wise. Poor scanning methods and varying soil conditions (moisture changes, e. g.) cause coins to be overlooked. Don't forget about newer, deeper-penetrating detectors that keep coming along. The new VLF types are getting down deeper than before. (See Chapter XX, "Understanding and Using the VLF.")

CHECK YOUR CHANGE. Ms. Norma Tinsley proves it is wise to check all your coins each time you get change from a purchase. She is holding a "blank" penny that she received in change. It is a genuine penny blank that made it all the way through one of the U. S. mints into her hands without being stamped with the likeness of Mr. Lincoln. Norma said that this was the first time she had ever known nothing to be worth something! Check your change, coin hunters!

| HIS | HERS |

Mr. and Mrs. Anthony Yero of Laurel, Maryland, have made many interesting finds during their coin hunting outings with their detectors. They each have their own detectors and keep a good, friendly game of competition going between themselves. As you can see from the pictures, they have their finds separated. If more families were to discover coin hunting the manufacturers of "Monopoly" might go out of business!

USE A RAKE TO GAIN ACCESS AND COINS!

Joseph W. Gehrke wrote to me explaining how his rake has paid off many times. When he travels, he carries an ordinary, short, steel tined garden rake. He thoroughly rakes all trashy areas before beginning to search with his detector. He said that the raking not only eliminates a lot of metallic junk but it also helps him find things and even gain access to some areas. In one ghost town in southern Arizona that was off-limits to TH'ers, he gained access when he told two ladies who worked there that he always raked and cleaned areas before searching, hauled off all debris, and never left telltale holes. The ladies became friendly with this volunteer yard cleaner and before the day was over Joseph left with plenty of good exercise, many late 1800 and early 1900 coins, and an invitation to come back!

In another area Joseph raked up a two-inch-long, 14K gold "cow" before he even brought out his detector. At an old abandoned railroad town he thoroughly raked and cleaned the entire area in front of the foundation of a train station. He then began detecting. Before all was said and done he came up with things like small Arizona tax tokens six to eight inches down, several rare date pennies and many other coins, including some forty-year-old Mexican coins in mint condition. Many of these things would have been "masked" and missed because of the iron junk had Joseph not first cleaned up with his rake! If we would all follow Joseph's cleaning suggestion, I believe we would be rewarded with greater finds not only today but also tomorrow when we are invited to come back.

DIG THEN GID!

Do you know what "GID" means? J. R. Rowland, writing in *The Nugget*, publication of the Oregon Treasure Hunters League, says that to retrieve most coins you must DIG first but then, quite logically, you should do the reverse, GID, after you have retrieved your coin. He says that our great hobby of coin hunting will suffer if even only one person does not fill his holes. How right he is! So, all coin and treasure hunters, heed J. R.'s excellent advice: DIG, THEN GID!

"COIN SHOOTERS' SPILL PATTERN"

An article by the above title by William D. Johnson immediately caught my attention when I saw it in TREA-SURE Magazine, Vol. 6, No. 9, September 1975. William and his wife, Donna, are to be praised for their novel idea, hard work and willingness to share their valuable information with all coin hunters. Thank you, William, and Bob Grant, Editor, TREASURE, for permission to reproduce the article in this revised edition of SUCCESS-FUL COIN HUNTING.

"Diversification is not just a descriptive word but a way of hunting to the successful coinshooter. In order to keep an even flow of coins, relics and jewelry coming in, he must carefully hunt the areas where people congregate. In short, the world is the coinshooter's arena, and quite a challenging one at that. The ground can consist of anything from sand to broken rock. The weather can be, and usually is, less than agreeable. Coins can be on the surface or, according to some coinshooters, 'elbow deep.' But there does seem to be one fairly common occurrence which can be depended upon to yield a find or two — the tree.

"Trees act like magnets to humans, partially because we are so dependent upon them, our standard of living not being able to exist otherwise. However, there is a less definable side to the tree, a romantic side. Is there anything more respectable than a huge old oak tree? Or more

The author and his wife, Donna, both experienced coin hunters, decided to see if there were a "pattern" to coins lost under shade trees.

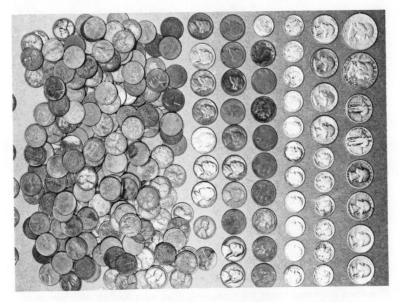

These fifty finds were the result of the spill-pattern experiment.

129

Our best find was a pink shell cameo ring from the early 1920's.

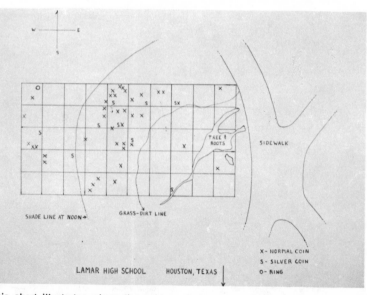

This chart illustrates where the coins and rings were located. (All four photographs courtesy William D. Johnson.)

fun? It is one of nature's playgrounds for all ages. As such, the area around each and every tree which may be standing guard over a lost coin should be diligently hunted.

"This author has had more than his share of good fortune while coinshooting underneath trees, especially with the recovery of silver coins. This good luck eventually led to the question as to whether a 'spill pattern' existed with lost coins. For example, the average coinshooter would expect coins to be more numerous as he approached the trunk of a tree. After all, the center of the tree would naturally be the center of activity. Or would it? It was this author's intention to establish whether a pattern actually existed and, if it did, to put that information to use both to speed up the hunt and increase the number of finds.

"The first problem was to find a tree which was suitable for study. One that had enough coins possibly to establish a pattern and yet still be relatively unhunted was a hard combination to find. However, just such a tree was located on the front lawn of Lamar Senior High School in Houston, Texas. The school was constructed in 1936 and the tree, an oak, seemed to be of about the same era. Several coinshooters, including myself, had attempted to hunt under the tree in question, only to be chased away by tin foil and pulltabs. But that was the key. We had all been chased away, leaving virtually untouched any coins and/or any patterns which might have developed.

"One of the two main problems, tin foil, was effectively defeated with the use of a discriminating detector. The other main problem, pulltabs, was not so easily done away with. The detector being used registered pulltabs and coins alike as 'good objects,' resulting in the necessity of digging all positive signals. Persistence was the unfortunate answer.

"With those two hunting problems out of the way, another one arose. Even if a pattern did exist, how would it be shown? The author decided to plot the recovered coins on a grid which could be mapped out underneath the tree with the use of some twine and stakes. A rectangular grid of fifteen feet by thirty feet was laid out. Then three-foot columns and rows were marked off, establishing fifty three-foot squares. The beginning of the grid started at the base of the tree and projected thirty feet underneath and away from the tree so as to give a fair representative sample of the area.

"With all of the preliminaries out of the way, the hunt began. One square at a time was thoroughly hunted, moving in rows from east to west. Each and every positive signal was dug up, even the obvious pulltabs. Two of those 'obvious pulltabs' turned out to be quarters, one silver. Each find, not including pulltabs, was accurately plotted on its representative square. Within completion of the second row, a very definite pattern began to emerge. Surprisingly, the vast majority of coins were being found between ten and fifteen feet from the tree trunk. As the hunt came to an end, the early pattern which had developed was very definitely established and confirmed.

"A total of 49 coins, one ring and 685 pulltabs was the reward for nine hours of backbreaking and knee-stiffening work. The coins and ring were as follows: 16 Lincoln wheatback cents, 1920-1957; 10 Lincoln Memorial cents, 1959-1973; 3 Jefferson nickels, 1946-1972; 5 Mercury dimes, 1925-1943; 1 Roosevelt dime, 1963; 3 Washington silver quarters, 1940-1944; 1 Washington clad quarter, 1973; 1 gold ring. Two of the finds deserve further mention. The 1940 Washington quarter was of the Denver mint, a semi-key coin grading in fine condition and valued at about two dollars. The gold ring was the best recovery, however. It was of the early 1920's era with an intact pink shell cameo. When a local antique dealer appraised it at over $100, my knees felt much better.

"Now, back to the original purpose of this article. Could the pattern which had shown up on the grid be utilized on future hunts? The answer would have to be a conditional 'yes.' First of all, it is evident that the conditions which resulted in a pattern under the tree in question are representative only to that particular tree. For example, this tree was frequented by high school students on their lunch break. The tree had a patch of dirt where the shade retarded the growth of grass and where the students would not sit for fear of getting their clothing dirty. It also had a shade line where grass did grow, permitting the students to sit on relatively clean grass and under the shade of the tree at the same time. The point is, this old oak tree did indeed have a 'spill pattern' due to certain conditions. Each and every tree will also have its own set of conditions, leaving it up to the individual coinshooter to interpret and translate those conditions into a successful hunt."

YOU NEED SOME CARDS

Several people, including Mr. R. C. Mills of Jackson, Tennessee, wrote in to note that many doors (or yards) were opened and that many good leads came along when printed business cards were handed out to owners of places where it was desired to search. Quite often coin or treasure hunters were permitted to search when otherwise they might not have been allowed to do so. Some property owners even told of other places where the hunting might be good. It is very hard for someone to refuse you when you hand that person a card with your name and address on it and a sentence something like, "I search with a metal detector for lost coins, jewelry and treasure. I promise not to destroy any property, to leave no holes unfilled and to leave the area just like I found it." Without question, an attractive business card adds class!

Mrs. Harold McCorkell is an avid coin hunter. She searches primarily for coins and other small jewelry lost in parks, playgrounds and other places where people have gathered. One day while searching in an old park area her detector produced a loud signal indicating a large buried object. She thought, "Surely this is an old tin can," and passed on by the object. Later, after thinking about the signal, she returned to the area and dug the object. This necklace is that object — an extremely rare and valuable Florentine necklace. One of the joys of treasure hunting is that you never know what you'll dig up next. Photo from author's book, TREASURE HUNTING PAYS OFF! by Ram Publishing Company.

EVEN THE GHOSTS ARE FRIENDLY HERE!

If you ever get to one of my favorite places, the Big Bend region of Southwest Texas, you can search an old ghost town to your heart's content. The ghost town of Terlingua is located on the road to Presidio, Texas, at the western boundary of Big Bend National Park. Seventy-five years ago Terlingua was a thriving mercury mining town; today only ghosts inhabit the hundreds of crumbled ruins. The owner of the ghost town, "Terlingua (Paul) Vonn," a prospector in his own right, has opened the town to all treasure hunters. Of course, that does not mean you can destroy the place or haul it off, but you can search the countless old buildings and ruins. "There must be thousands of coins and other lost things there," says "Terlingua Vonn." Long before the detector was invented the old mud roofs fell in, covering what was buried or lost beneath the floors of the many homes and businesses. These things are still there, awaiting the detector operator. If you are ever in Southwest Texas stop in to see "Terlingua Vonn" at his store on the highway near the western entrance to Big Bend National Park. Try to make it during Terlingua's annual World Championship Chili Cook-Off, held in October. Held now for more than ten years, the Cook-off attracts the occupants of as many as 2,500 motor homes, trailers and vans, plus the chili purists who come to this spooky mining camp from all over the hemisphere. "It's a good place to retire, too," says Vonn. "There are uncounted thousands of acres of land available. A man couldn't explore it all in a lifetime!" Thanks, Vonn, for the invitation. (Get permission from Vonn <u>before</u> you dig!

I wish everyone could find a toy bank, with its coins, like this one.

A VERY INFORMATIVE BOOK

Just before going to press with this revised edition of SUCCESSFUL COIN HUNTING I received a copy of Warren Merkitch's new book, BEACHCOMBER'S HANDBOOK, $5.00, published by Exanimo Press, Box 8, Segundo, Colorado 81070. Each of the book's 47 large (8"x10½") pages contains good and specific information on recovering

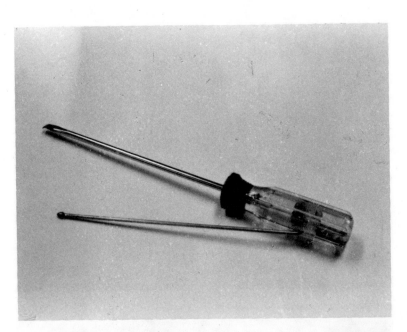

My thanks to Wayne Fess, New Albany, Indiana, for sending information about this combination screwdriver-probe that he designed. Note the end is bent to facilitate coin removal. The probe is hinged so that it lies flat against the screwdriver for storage in a sheath or it can be pulled out at a 90°-angle to push into the ground to locate detected coins. A small round magnet is set into a hole drilled in the handle end. The magnet helps Wayne to locate tiny pieces of iron that sometimes are almost impossible to find. A good design, Wayne! We appreciate your telling us about your idea.

jewelry, coins and other valuables from ocean beaches and lake and river fronts. Detailed instructions are included for building a dry and a wet sifter to use in recovery work. You should consider Mr. Merkitch's sifter as a convenient and efficient companion to your metal detector when searching for valuables on a beach or waterfront area. Illustrations depict, among other things, typical lake and ocean beach profiles and a suggested metal detector search plan. The nine chapters include practical, useful information and instruction on various techniques of beachcombing, such as using a metal detector, dry and wet sifting, and lake and river sifting. One chapter is devoted to a discussion of how the weather can affect not only the configuration of a beach but also where and how you should search for valuables. Mr. Merkitch's many years of experience are evident in his HANDBOOK; he no doubt knows whereof he speaks. If you are going to go beachcombing, you should have the BEACHCOMBER'S HANDBOOK.

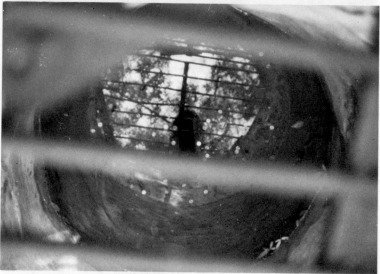

Ah, those wishing wells! The boy in the top photo is probably wishing for the coins he sees in the well (bottom photo), but I wonder what the girl is wishing for? Grizelda, a young girl from South Texas, smiles as she tells visitors how many coins are tossed into the well each year. The number is staggering! Let this picture story guide you. How many water places throughout the United States contain countless old coins thrown there by people of all ages as they wished for the things of life that they wanted so badly and hoped the "tossed coin" would bring them their wish?

136

You've heard the Mother Goose children's rhyme which begins, "There was a crooked man who went a crooked mile. He found a crooked sixpence against a crooked stile."? This story came about as a result of a crooked coin. During the 17th century in Northern England a yearly fair was held. Sometime during this period an unusual practice came into play. If a man liked a particular lady and wanted to marry her, he would bend a sixpence and give the coin to her. If she wanted to marry the fellow, she would keep the coin; if not, she would throw it away. During a recent coin hunting trip to the fair site, Frank Mellish of London, England, found one of the discarded sixpence coins as shown in the photo, thus lending credence to the belief that the nursery rhyme began as a result of an historical event.

"HOW TO FIND THOSE OVERLOOKED COINS"

Thus read the title of an article by Dave Scott which appeared in the January 1976 issue of TREASURE Magazine. Dave Scott has been able to turn up many valuable old coins in areas other coinshooters thought had been thoroughly worked out. He says bottle caps, tin cans, and other junk can actually be a coin hunter's best friend — they keep other treasure hunters from finding all the coins. Bob Grant, Editor of TREASURE, published Dave's article telling how easy it was to find coins overlooked by others. The article was so interesting and informative I asked for permission to reproduce portions here. I thank Dave and Bob for their generous permission to do so.

"I'd been searching the ancient reunion places and fairgrounds very systematically, but it was mid-summer and nearing midday. So I retreated from the brain-frying heat of the Texas sun to seek refuge in the sparse shade of a dying oak. It had once been a magnificent tree. Possibly 80 years ago its shade had attracted visitors like a magnet. It took little imagination to envision families camped under its branches, playing dominoes, pitching horseshoes, and maybe dropping a coin or two.

"If, indeed, those visitors of decades ago did drop coins, chances were most of them had already been found by coin hunters who preceded me. Like most county-owned reunion and fairgrounds open to the public, this one had been hunted to a bloody froth. In fact, someone remarked that the only coins I'd find on this reunion ground were those dropped by other coinshooters. In essence, I was searching for coins 'where they weren't.'

"Still, with the hope of finding coins the others had overlooked, I began searching slowly with my Garrett BFO Discriminator. Close against the base of the tree I encountered several negative signals. I crossed more junk as I worked toward the edge of the shade. Moving over a couple of steps, I began working back toward the trunk.

"Suddenly my Discriminator screamed as my meter indicated a huge piece of junk. I backed off, then cautiously probed close to the big signal. Then I heard it — a faint 'round' signal just inches from the edge of the junk. I swept the coil over the spot again, watching the discriminating meter. It registered a clear 'good' indication even though the signal was extremely weak. I jabbed my digging knife into the ground and pried out the piece of junk — a flattened can a couple of inches down. Then I checked the signal again. It sounded good.

" 'Could be a .22 case,' I told myself, preparing for possible disappointment. I plunged my knife into the loose soil created by year after year of decaying leaves and wedged out a three-inch-deep plug. I pressed the plug against the coil. No signal. I checked the hole, and there it was. The lovely faint signal was still deeper. It couldn't be a .22 case.

"Backing off a safe three inches or so from the spot where I'd pinpointed the signal, I carefully worked the knife blade deep into the soil and began applying pressure. The plug broke out beautifully and tumbling from it came the unmistakable form of a silver dime. Exposed from its coating of dirt was part of an encircling wreath. I very gently flaked off a portion of loose dirt. It was a Barber dime, a 1911-D in beautiful shape.

"It wasn't the best coin I'd found, not by a long shot. However, I got a special kick out of it because once again I'd found a good coin in an area I was told had been 'worked out.'

"The truth is, out of that same 'worked out' reunion and fairground I had already found about 30 wheat pennies, many in the early teens; four Indianhead pennies as early as 1898; eight 'V' nickels, including an 1896; about a dozen buffalo nickels, most with high dates and some earlier than 1920; six Mercury dimes dating back to a beautiful 1917-S; and six lovely old Barber dimes, including an 1893-S.

"In the process of tapping this 'worked out' reunion ground for those old fine coins, I've learned some lessons which could prove helpful to other coin hunters faced with the problem of hunting public areas such as old reunion grounds and parks which have already been heavily searched. Making these techniques work depends largely on the use of a good discriminator because, as you will see, searching around junk figures largely in the plan. Nevertheless, armed with these suggested techniques, a lot of patience and a discriminator, chances are you're going to be rewarded with coins. If you're like me, you'll get twice the kick out of finding coins that have been missed by other coin hunters as you would if you found them in virgin territory.

"In an area that's been overrun by coin hunters junk becomes your best friend. That's because junk discourages careful searching and camouflages coin signals.

"For example, take the Barber dime I described finding. For decades it had been protected by the rusty old can so close to it. In effect, that can had protected an area the size of a ten-gallon hat. Theoretically, several coins could have been concealed there. Remember, too, the area under a tree must be considered among the best real estate for lost coins in this or any other reunion ground or park. With these facts in mind, searching carefully around the can was a highly logical thing to do. One day this winter I plan to return to this tree, dig up all the junk around it and search the cleaned out area carefully for coins.

"Another interesting condition exists on this particular reunion ground which must be similar to others. Scattered over it are patches almost solid with ancient bottlecaps. These rusty relics apparently mark the locations of long-gone soda pop stands. And bless them, I'm certain those bottle tops protect many, many valuable old coins. After all, a lot of money changed hands right where those old caps fell.

"So how do you find coins in a pile of litter like this? Well, it ain't easy, but at least you know they're there. The trick is to search for nooks and crannies that are devoid of caps and to hunt just around the perimeter of the junk. The smaller the search coil, the better. The small coil lets you isolate coins from caps more frequently because if the coil detects a bottle cap and a coin at the same time the discrimination signal is either neutralized or registered 'bad.' With a small coil you'll come closer to isolating a coin without picking up the signal of a cap, thereby producing a 'good' discriminating signal.

"One of the big advantages of my Garrett BFO Discriminator is that I've rigged it to accept other coils. While the standard 6-inch coil is good for the bottle cap patches, a new 3½-inch coil I've just acquired will be even better.

"If you're long on patience and energy, here's another way to attack the pile of bottle tops. Systematically clean out an area, removing both the caps and the coins. It goes without saying that an excavation of this type should be carefully smoothed back. Holes should never be left, even in the remotest part of a little-used reunion ground or park.

"Brush can also be productive in a heavily hunted area. Most coinshooters scan the outskirts of a bush, but few take the time and trouble to probe carefully in heavy foliage. Keeping in mind that a bush may not have been there years ago, search every bit of it you can, just like it was the best place in the whole area . . . because it just might be.

"This fact became apparent as I was hunting a remote area of the ancient reunion ground. I had worked this area hard, but had not found a single coin. Because there was a good layer of soil I figured the coins must be deep. Most of the reunion ground consists of a rocky shelf covered by a thin layer of soil.

"As I scanned this barren section it suddenly dawned on me that there was an absence of junk. Any metal indication would stand out like a sore thumb. Apparently the area truly had been virtually worked out. As I contemplated this dreary development my eyes fell on a nearby mesquite surrounded by scrub brush. I began working around and under it carefully, jabbing my coil in every small opening. Near the base of the mesquite I got an unusually strong signal which registered good on the discriminator. In went my knife and out came a shallow 1920-D buffalo nickel with the date so high I could read it through the dirt. On the opposite side of the tree I received another strong signal. It was a wheat penny, also a 1920-D.

"I spent the remainder of the afternoon hunting in bushes, searching high grass and probing around large rocks. I found enough coins to make it all worthwhile, including a 1903-O Barber dime so beautifully preserved it has to be extra fine.

"Another type of area commonly neglected by the

average coin hunter is the roads inside old reunion grounds and parks, especially if they've been graveled and are packed so hard you almost need a hammer and chisel.

"In the reunion ground I hunt I find good old coins right under a layer of peagravel in the roads. Sure, it's tough digging, but the coins are there. I can't recall finding one coin I thought had been damaged by 'traffic.'

"Another productive area is the ground immediately adjacent to the road. For some reason, coin hunters apparently have a tendency to give roads a wide berth. So keep in mind the importance of looking where they don't.

"The greatest lesson I've learned from hunting the old reunion ground and others like it is to hunt slowly. When I say, "slowly," I mean really slowly. Those faint signals that sound like ground effect or your imagination are the ones that count. And, unfortunately, you'll pass a lot of them by unless you literally creep.

"This fact was driven home to me when I first began hunting the old reunion ground. The first half-dozen times I worked it, I combed several areas and found absolutely nothing. Like most other coin hunters, I worked hurriedly, figuring that the more ground I covered, the more I'd find. Nothing could have been farther from the truth.

"One morning I was hurrying my way across an area where a steam-driven merry-go-round had once stood. Suddenly I thought I detected a signal slightly different from the slight ground effect in the area. I swept the coil over the spot very, very slowly. This time I heard the faint signal distinctly — much too small to be ground effect.

"With good cooperation from the meter, I began digging. At a depth of perhaps 5 inches I unearthed a beautiful old 'V' nickel. Taking the lesson to heart, I continued moving at a snail's pace. Perhaps five feet from the hole I'd just dug, I detected another very weak signal — a carbon copy of the first. Incredibly, it was another 'V' nickel about as deep as the other. Continuing to hunt in slow motion, I found more deep coins. I pulled them out in areas I'd already hunted. I found them where everyone else had undoubtedly hunted.

"Since then, I've adopted an attitude that keeps me moving slowly and intensifies my concentration. I hunt each area of ground as though I had every reason to believe it held more deep coins than any other. No longer do I move hurriedly, going through the motions of searching an area while sizing up another that looks better. I'm finding more good, deep coins than ever before.

"What it all boils down to is this: there are good coins left in those 'worked out' areas. To find them you have to hunt a little more thoroughly, a little more slowly, and a little smarter.

"Sure, it takes a lot of patience, but finding valuable old coins is a heckuva lot better than not finding valuable old coins. Right?"

Thank you, Dave Scott, for this very valuable information.

Dave Scott is using his new techniques to find those overlooked coins. At the tip of the knife is the unmistakable shape of a silver dime. It was very deep and surrounded by ancient bottle caps. Photo by Byron Scott.

CHAPTER XVI

People Who Coin Hunt

I have met many successful coin hunters. In all cases, they are down-to-earth people who enjoy being in the great outdoors pursuing the hobbies they love. They are successful not only because of the countless things they find but also because coin hunting has broadened their horizons and provided them with a meaningful spare time activity.

In this revision of SUCCESSFUL COIN HUNTING I decided to include a brief "life story" or description of a successful coin hunting method of several of these people. Some started coin hunting young in life; some started long after they were married and had families. In each case, however, they proved coin hunting is a very rewarding hobby . . . one that everyone can enjoy!

RICHARD SMART

Exploration and discovery are a great part of what treasure hunting is all about. Most of us would like to believe we are intrepid hunters and explorers; many of us have discovered varied and sundry treasures . . . but none more rare than the 1776 Continental dollar recently dug up by Richard Smart of Oklahoma.

Richard, using his five-year-old Garrett Hunter BFO, found the pewter Continental dollar at a depth of about ten inches near the center of an old rock corral in Seminole County. The discovery was a great thrill for the treasure hunting hobbyist, especially when he was shown a magazine report that a previously found Continental dollar was worth $12,000! The Continental dollar, struck in silver, pewter and brass, probably in Philadelphia, was the first dollar size coin ever proposed for the United States, though it never reached general circulation. The old pewter coin points up the fact that the Colonists were hard pressed for precious metals in those early days of independence. Richard's dollar is well preserved, with the words and date plainly visible.

Previously, the enthusiastic young treasure hunter found a cache of 1880's coins with a face value of $300. They were buried rather deeply in an old crock near a house which has been abandoned for over fifty years. In the same area he has found single coins dated before 1900.

Richard, who has been treasure hunting for about ten

In the top photograph Richard Smart (right) holds the 1776 pewter Continental dollar which could be worth as much as $12,000. He recently found the coin with his five-year-old Garrett Hunter. A close-up of the coin is shown in the lower photo. The coins and other things arranged on the cloth in front of Richard represent a portion of the results of his coin hunting activities, as well as a large cache of coins he also recently discovered. He has been very successful in all of his coin and treasure hunting activities. Time and time again it has been proved that research is one of the most important aspects of successful coin and treasure hunting. Lloyd Parsons (left) is a long-time treasure hunter. He has many of his treasure finds and artifacts on display in various parts of the ghost town type buildings you can see in the background. Lloyd owns and operates Territory Town (near Okemah, Oklahoma), an attraction popular with tourists and campers during the summer months .

years, predicts that with the new Garrett detectors he ". . . can find a lot more," adding that, "I think I can make a living money hunting," with the instruments.

BILL BOSH

When Bill Bosh flew out of Perth, Australia in late 1980, he was lugging about $100,000-worth of gold in his luggage, all of it found with a metal detector.

Bill, former dealer coordinator for Garrett Metal Detectors, found the nuggets during a stay in Australia to train Garrett dealers and customers in the best ways to use Garrett detectors for electronic prospecting.

For Bill, who carries a reputation as a top professional coin hunter, the thrill of his stay Down Under was the uncovering of a 152-ounce specimen in the Mt. Magnet area. The nugget, which contained 64.5 ounces of gold, was worth more than $60,000 as a collector's piece.

"I'll never forget that day," Bill recalled. "It took my friend and me eight hours to dig down through two feet of solid rock to where the nugget was located, but, boy . . . was it worth it!"

That was on Bill's third trip to Western Australia. On the previous one, he found over 100 ounces. On the first journey, he uncovered a rare gold crystal, weighing 5.3 grams. He was immediately offered $1,500 for it as a specimen, but declined the offer.

Bill started treasure hunting in his early twenties, primarily digging bottles. Since the late 1960's, he has been deeply involved in coin and cache hunting.

"I guess I've had some luck, but I've also worked hard in making good finds," he says. Bill was referring to a cache of gold coins, three other small money caches, and a wide variety of rare coins of all denominations he has found.

He loves to search old home yards and enjoys working areas that others have already searched to try to find the deeper stuff that they've missed.

Another favorite pastime is traveling to treasure hunts and walking off with assorted prizes. "Making new friends and meeting old ones at these events also means a lot to me," Bill says.

While gold fever seems to drive a lot of people crazy, it doesn't appear to affect Bill that way. He nonchalantly describes his gold hunting as ". . . a great way to relax." He considers his hobby as a sideline to his main job of selling detectors.

"I'm not in prospecting for the money," he claims. "I do it because I enjoy it."

145

Bill Bosh poses with the 152-ounce gold specimen he found in Western Australia.

ERNIE CURLEE

Ernie "Carolina" Curlee, Charlotte, North Carolina, has written some very inspiring words about how he and his family first became interested in metal detectors and coin hunting. It all began, he said, when his son, David, asked for a metal detector for his twelfth Christmas. Ernie said he thought this would be just another gadget for David and that it would go the way of other discarded toys, but David's new gadget soon got the whole family interested in what became for them their first togetherness hobby.

David got his detector that Christmas. In fact, he received his gift Christmas Eve. Thirty minutes later he and his dad had dug several holes in the backyard and found a few coins. Three days later his dad took him to a schoolyard not far from their home to do some searching. When it began to rain and they started to leave, Ernie said, "Let me try that thing." While walking toward the car Ernie got a buzz on the detector. He cut a plug of soil and dug up a gold charm bracelet worth about $250. He has been hooked ever since. Three weeks later he bought a detector for himself and by March the following year he decided to inquire about becoming a metal detector dealer, adding another product to those handled by his company already in operation.

Ernie and David spent a lot of time treasure hunting through the summer, having good success with coin hunting. They found, among other things, one ring with seven diamonds. They even journeyed to a Prospectors Club Hunt in Lebanon, Indiana. Thirty days later, in October 1974, Ernie sponsored The Carolina Treasure Hunt and later, The Southern Championship Treasure Hunt in 1975 and 1976. His other son, Tim, who is ten years old, and his wife, Iris, soon became interested in treasure hunting. Together the entire family has visited organized treasure hunts in Virginia, Massachusetts, North Carolina, Oklahoma and Indiana, covering about 20,000 miles "... pursuing this crazy, wonderful hobby of treasure hunting and camping. We always have four to eight detectors with us on these trips. We have journeyed north to Canada and west to Cripple Creek, Colorado; we have covered Civil War battlefields in North Carolina, South Carolina, Mississippi and Virginia. Treasure hunting is a crazy hobby, but it is a beautiful kind of crazy that creates friendships that will last for a lifetime, a companionship with your family, and a nearly indefinable something that puts you in touch with history in a way that no other hobby could do."

"Carolina Ernie" Curlee and his son, David, display in their shop some of the coins, tokens, and jewelry they have found. What started out to be only the purchase of a "gadget" detector for David when he was twelve has led this family into a very serious family sport that pays dividends. The lower photo shows some of the rings and jewelry found by the Curlee family. "Carolina Ernie" has written a fascinating book that is a must for all persons who use metal detectors. The book, THE COMPLETE BOOK OF COMPETITION TREASURE HUNTING, published by Ram Publishing Company, should be in every treasure hunter's library.

148

DINO ROSSI

My thanks again to Editor Bob Grant of TREASURE Magazine for permitting me to reproduce portions of the following article about Dino Rossi. The article ("Seattle Teenager Finds Park Treasures") appeared in the August 1976 TREASURE. Dino is another young man who has found joys and successes that stem from coin and treasure hunting. Even before this article appeared in TREASURE Magazine, I had heard about Dino's successes. We thank him for telling his story. Keep up the good work, Dino!

"Teenager Dino Rossi had a flourishing candle business two years ago when he discovered treasure hunting and decided that was the hobby — and the enterprise — he wanted to spend all of his free time doing.

"Rossi, who lives in a suburb of Seattle, Washington, had saved more than $200 from his candle business when an issue of TREASURE FOUND's sister publication, TREASURE, caught his attention.

"He thought, 'Gee, these cats are really finding stuff. I could make some money this way.'

"So the resourceful young Rossi withdrew his savings and bought a metal detector. Since then he has found hundreds of coins — old and recent, numerous pieces of jewelry, trade tokens, antique bottles and an old revolver.

"He has also become one of the most ardent treasure hunters in his local area, and his interest in TH'ing has expanded to include all aspects of the hobby as well as coinshooting. Yet his enjoyment in dredging for gold and exploring old mines doesn't exclude his continued enjoyment and success in coinshooting.

" 'It took me three days to find my first quarter,' recalls the teenager. 'It took that long for me to learn how to use my new Garrett Coin Hunter. I'd never even seen a metal detector before.'

"From that meager beginning, Rossi quickly proved he could move on to more lucrative TH'ing. One of his prime hunting grounds — and a favorite detecting spot for many Seattle TH'ers — is Luna Park, site of an old amusement park on the shore of Lake Washington. The park was closed down in the early 1900's. In recent years the location where it once stood has proved a fertile detecting spot.

" 'I only started working Luna last April,' says Rossi. 'Already I've found three V-nickels, three Barber dimes, a Seated-Liberty dime, several Mercury dimes and Indian-head pennies, and a German-made .22 cal. revolver. It's what they call a 'Saturday Night Special,' but one of the better makes.'

149

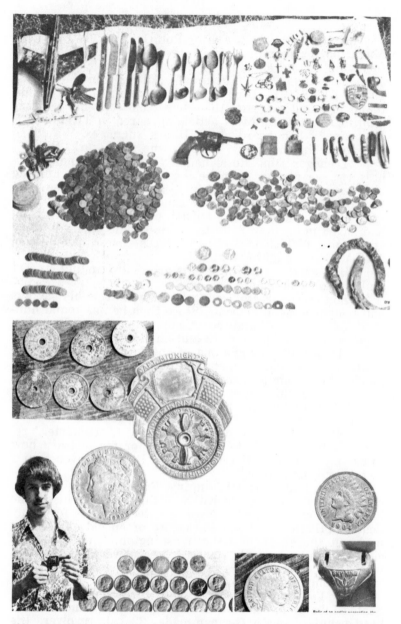

After five fruitless trips to Seattle's Luna Park, persistent Dino's sixth trip yielded two V nickels. Since Dino gave up his after-school candle business, he has found that treasure hunting can be a profitable hobby, as evidenced by the past year's successes.

150

"As most determined Seattle TH'ers do, Rossi studies the tidal actions that affect the hunting grounds he plans to cover at Luna.

" 'I usually work after a storm and during a minus tide. It seems the bigger the storm the better the hunting — more treasure is uncovered. Then with a good low tide the sand really shifts and sometimes it brings a lot of new goodies. I've even found a roller skate from the old roller-rink. Unfortunately it was set aside and forgotten. I was never able to locate it again.'

"After school and on weekends Rossi packs his detector over his shoulder and heads for areas more accessible than the once popular Luna Park.

" 'I hit most of the nearby parks and schoolyards. In the parks I like to detect places where people lie down — off the beaten track. I just watch where people seem to be.'

"It was in Seattle's Volunteer Park that Rossi discovered his first ring, a handcrafted sterling silver and jade ring worth more than $50. The ring wasn't the only find from that particular park. Another expedition netted 35 coins and more jewelry. Parks have been good to Rossi as one of his favorite finds — an old silver dollar — was found in King County Park.

"Old houses are another of Rossi's primary hunting grounds. 'My Dad and I drive around and look for these older houses. We usually check the front yard but mostly search the side yards. Often we'll go back after one of them has been torn down. It's especially good hunting after they take out some of the grass and shrubbery.'

"One of Rossi's prime finds was a valuable 1928 Barber dime located at the site of an old house where the topsoil had been removed. 'It was still down about six inches,' says Dino.

"Parks, Luna Park, schools and old houses have netted Rossi more than coins. He also boasts an impressive collection of tokens that have resulted from his detecting. Included in his cache are local tokens — some worth more than $5 each — and interesting tax tokens.

" 'They were originally worth one-third-cent and date from around 1935,' explains the resourceful teenager. 'They were made of aluminum — at least the ones that we find are. At one time the same tokens were made of a fiber-board-like substance, but those have disintegrated or they just can't be found with detectors. Even the aluminum ones have cardboard cores and were sometimes used for buttons, washers and so on. The tokens were the state's way of getting its portion of the one-percent sales tax.'

"The adventure and success he has had in metal detecting only served to whet the youngster's TH'ing appetite. Since the purchase of his first detector two years ago, young Rossi and his family have all joined the Cascade Treasure Hunting Club and are active participants in the activities of the group.

" 'Dino and his Mother gave me my detector — a Garrett Money Hunter TR — for Christmas,' says the senior Rossi. 'Up to that time Dino did all the detecting and I did all the digging!

" 'Now I get to do a little detecting on my own. We quite often work with only one detector because we still find it pretty fast to have one person digging while the other is detecting and marking the detected points with screwdrivers. We share the fun rather than competing.'

"Sharing and working faithfully at their hobby has proved lucrative for the Rossis — not only on the amount of treasures they've found — but in the enjoyment they've gained.

"And young Dino says he doesn't miss the candle business for a minute!"

THE STULLERS

Frank Stuller and his wife, Carol, are a most charming and interesting couple who combine motorhome traveling with their intriguing, profitable hobby and leisure time activity — treasure hunting. Since Frank retired from his job in 1970, they have traveled rather extensively from their home in Wisconsin visiting motorhome rallies, friends and relatives over a wide area of the country, coin and treasure hunting as they go. Frank and Carol were introduced to treasure hunting a few years after he retired when they came across some brochures on metal detecting. They felt that it would be a hobby quite compatible with traveling. The Stullers knew that reliable detecting instruments were a "must" so in order to decide what equipment they would purchase they talked with many owners of detectors to find out the qualities that make up a good detector.

Since cold weather in Wisconsin limits coin hunting to about seven months a year, a good part of the remaining months are spent on the road, searching for treasure legends and areas. In their travels they have hunted from the poolsides of plush Las Vegas casinos to remote ghost towns, never failing to come up with finds. The Stullers travel in excess of 10,000 miles a year and have treasure hunted from New York to Florida to California and points between. In one area they found 270 coins in less than two hours! They find city officials and police very cooperative

152

with regard to coin hunting in public places when permission is sought first, and they are most careful to leave no marks or holes where they search and dig.

Watch for the Stullers . . . when you find them I'll bet they will have a pocket full of old, dirty (but valuable) coins!

Frank and Carol Stuller enjoy their free time traveling around the United States and Canada. Since their retirement, they have found that coin hunting fills in much of their free time quite successfully. They travel great distances to attend treasure hunting meets and motor home rallies. "Regardless of where we go," say the Stullers, "we always find good places to coin hunt!"

Here is just a small portion of the coins and countless other things Frank and Carol Stuller have found. There are few states where the Stullers have not found coins and other valuables. It has been estimated that the total wealth found by all treasure hunters in the United States amounts to at least one million dollars per month, a figure probably lower than the actual amount.

DR. JACK R. TRAMMELL

Since 1971, Dr. Trammell, former Assistant Superintendent of the Lancaster School District in Texas, has searched and treasure hunted old homesites, fence rows, barns and vacant lots and has perfected his coin hunting technique around schoolgrounds' close at hand. His enthusiasm and exuberance are contagious! Dr. Trammell certainly adds great credibility to the fast growing outdoor sport and recreational activity of treasure hunting.

On the occasion of my first meeting with Dr. Trammell, he came by the office with a heavily-laden carrying case containing coins, pistols, knives and other objects which he and Al Levulis, his partner from Fort Worth, have jointly discovered. Behind a building they found a pistol buried with six fifty-caliber slugs. Two knives were found inside an old stump. They decided to flip a coin to see who would win both knives . . . and Dr. Trammell won. He gives the impression of being a lucky person, but, more importantly, he is a hard worker in something he really likes and believes in. Having seen many of the items he has found, I have no doubt that the old adage, seek and you shall find, has come true for him.

Dr. Trammell gives a lot of credit to his trusted partner, Al, with whom he plans and works on every project. Together they've been to some very interesting places, one of which was a deserted farm where they became curious about blazes carved into each of a line of trees near a house which had been the home of an old hermit. There were eight such trees near the house and at the foot of each blaze-marked tree they found small containers of old coins. One of the most exciting finds was a Blake and Co., Assayers, $20 gold piece. Also found were two $5 and two $10 Republic of Texas paper currency bills, one 1806 British coin and an 1838 U. S. penny.

Dr. Trammell stresses one thing . . . research, research, research! Do your homework, he says, and your scores will jump sharply! He couldn't ask for a better partner; half of everything he finds goes to the Lord.

THANK YOU

My thanks to all of you who permitted me to write about you in this book. It is my hope that your successes and experiences will help others as they pursue our great hobby of coin hunting.

154

Dr. Trammell came over to the office one day and brought a few of his most recent finds, displayed on the table. He has been successful in both coin and treasure hunting because he does his home work! (See text.)

Many coin and treasure hunters prefer the smallest, lightest weight detector for full time use and/or as their back-up unit. Several manufacturers build this type detector. The particular model shown here, a C & G Technology detector, is a good example of this type of equipment. With the control handle located between the control box and the searchcoil, good balance, an easy swing, and a lightweight feel is achieved.

CHAPTER XVII

Types of Detectors Coin Hunters Can Use

While some detector types are especially designed for coin hunting, other types designed for universal, general purpose applications can also be used to search for coins. In fact, practically every type of portable detector manufactured can be used for coin hunting.

Major types used by coin hunters are, in alphabetical order: the Automatic Ground Elimination (Discrimination), Beat Frequency Oscillator (BFO), Pulse Induction, Transmitter-Receiver (TR), and Very Low Frequency (VLF). The descriptions below give a general idea of the capabilities of each type; following chapters discuss them in greater detail.

AUTOMATIC
GROUND ELIMINATION DETECTORS

Automatic Ground Elimination detectors are near the top of the coin hunter's preferred instrument list. When correctly designed and manufactured, this detector type is the easiest to use and ranks extremely high in coin hunting capability. Most Automatic Ground Elimination detectors are built especially and exclusively for coin hunting, even though some manufacturers claim their models can be used for other hunting applications as well. Be cautioned, however, that this detector type is not the most suitable for all kinds of treasure hunting and electronic prospecting. Nevertheless, for the person interested primarily or solely in coin hunting, the Automatic Ground Elimination detector could very well be the best choice.

BFO DETECTORS

Beat frequency oscillator (BFO) detectors have been used by coin hunters for at least thirty years and there are probably many thousands of these instruments still in use today. A BFO is an extremely universal detector that can be used effectively in all phases of treasure hunting, even though it does not have ground elimination and the depth capability of other types. When properly designed, a quality built BFO is very capable in many applications, including coin hunting, and is certainly a joy to use, but it must rank last in the coin hunter's preference.

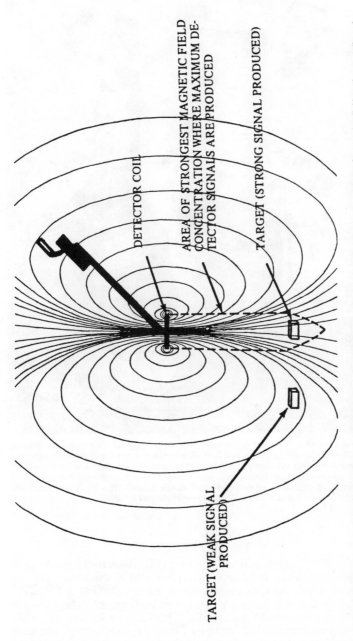

DETECTOR COIL

AREA OF STRONGEST MAGNETIC FIELD CONCENTRATION WHERE MAXIMUM DETECTOR SIGNALS ARE PRODUCED

TARGET (STRONG SIGNAL PRODUCED)

TARGET (WEAK SIGNAL PRODUCED)

This illustration represents the electromagnetic field lines and resultant detection pattern produced by a detector's searchcoil. Note the crowding of the field lines directly beneath the searchcoil. It is this crowding that causes metallic targets to be detected primarily beneath the searchcoil within the detection pattern as outlined by the dashed lines.

157

George Mroczkowski, President of the San Diego Gem and Treasure Hunting Association; Charles Garrett; Dr. Richard Fales; and John Quade, stage, screen, and television actor, talk about treasure hunting and a film about treasure hunting which they made. The film is available, free of charge, to all clubs and groups who want to view it. You'll enjoy this film that was written, filmed, produced, and acted out exclusively by treasure hunters. Write to Garrett Electronics, 2814 National Drive, Garland, Texas 75041, to schedule your showing.

TR DETECTORS

Like BFO's, transmitter-receiver (TR) detectors have been in use for many years and many, many are still in use today. During the years when the only choice was between BFO or a TR, TR's were often the coin hunter's preferred instrument. They are not capable of performing all treasure hunting tasks and are definitely not recommended for most forms of prospecting, but they are highly capable detectors which detect coins quite deeply.

They do not have ground canceling capability and their use is very restricted in mineralized areas. TR's are still manufactured, primarily as inexpensive detectors, and now rank very low on the coin hunter's preference list because they are other, newer types which are much more capable.

PULSE INDUCTION DETECTORS

Pulse induction detectors have certainly come into their own in the past two or three years and are especially preferred by those who work ocean beaches and other salt water locations. They are virtually mandatory in salt water areas where black magnetic sand is present. While nothing prevents thepulse from being used in fresh water areas and on dry land, other types of detectors, such as the Automatic Ground Elimination and certain VLF types, are preferred. The pulse is, without question, the over-all Number One choice of the ocean beach coin and treasure hunter, but it is not recommended for prospecting.

VLF DETECTORS

Very low frequency (VLF) detectors have, for many years, been the preferred coin hunting instruments, though many coin hunters are now turning to the Automatic Ground Elimination type. Certain VLF's are capale of performing every treasure hunting and prospecting task and there are many variations of the VLF type: the VLF all-metal, VLF/TR, VLF/VLF Trash Elimination (discrimination), and the VLF/Automatic Ground Elimination (discrimination). Quality VLF's rank on an equal footing with the best automatic ground elimination detectors. A choice between the two is decided perhaps by such considerations as the fact that VLF types utilize manual ground canceling and VLF design characteristics make it more suited for universal all-around hunting. Some VLF models, however, have a true AUTOMATIC Ground Elimination mode.

WHAT PRICE TO PAY?

Of the many factors to consider in selecting a detector for coin hunting, price is one you should certainly take into account. The best guide is to determine how much you want to spend and then to choose an instrument in that price range. You might use as a further guideline something like the recommendation concerning the purchase of a house or car: buy one that is slightly above what you think you can afford.

You can count on the fact that, unlike a house or a car, your detector will pay for itself. How quickly depends upon you! If you spend a few dollars more to get a high quality, versatile instrument that is the most suited to your expected requirements, in all probabiility the extra expense will prove worthwhile. Too many times persons using inadequate detectors pass over coins worth several times the cost of the best coin hunting detector.

On the other hand, do not make the mistake of purchasing the most expensive detector, thinking that you are buying the best detector for your needs. Some instruments are priced at what it seems the market will bear, a cost not necessarily related to competitive models, quality, or function.

Do your research. The best detector for you is the one that meets your particular requirements. Quality and performance can be found at most price levels. Make a diligent effort to locate the best combination of quality, performance, and versatility at a price that suits your budget.

(Editor's note. For a complete analysis of the major types of metal detectors, read the author's book, MODERN METAL DETECTORS, published by Ram Books.)

CHAPTER XVIII

Understanding and Using Automatic Ground Elimination Detectors

Automatic Ground Elimination coin hunting detectors perform as the name indicates; that is, they automatically eliminate detection of iron earth minerals, a capability that makes them very easy to use. About all the operator has to do is turn the detector on, maybe press a button, and start operating. No adjustments are ever needed for eliminating detection effects of iron earth minerals.

In addition to their automatic capability, these detectors are designed to detect coins to extreme depths. They give a pronounced, very sharp, well defined signal on coins and operate either silently or with slight threshold audio.

AVOID CONFUSION

The automatic feature of this detector type should not be confused with the automatic TUNING feature found on many TR and VLF types. The automatic ground elimination circuitry senses the presence of iron earth minerals beneath the searchcoil and automatically adjusts the detector to eliminate detection of the minerals so that no control adjustments are necessary.

Automatic TUNING as found on certain TR's and VLF's automatically keeps the audio TUNING level at a pre-determined point. Automatic tuning does not automatically adjust detector circuitry to eliminate the detection effects of iron earth minerals. As an added bonus, some Automatic Ground Elimination detector types ALSO automatically keep the audio at the pre-determined silent or faint threshold level.

A FURTHER NOTE

All Automatic Ground Elimination detectors may not have true ability to eliminate or cancel earth minerals. At this writing, at least one manufacturer claims to have a detector that automatically cancels ground minerals, but testing proves otherwise. That company's detector is factory adjusted to ignore minerals of only one given density. Mineral densities that vary from the norm will not be ignored.

Also be aware that some manufacturers may give their detector models names that IMPLY that the detectors have automatic ground elimination characteristics when actually they do not.

CAPABILITIES

Automatic ground elimination circuitry is optimized specifically for coin hunting; thus, it is necessary that these instruments be used primarily in that application. While some manufacturers claim their automatic ground elimination detectors are suitable for prospecting, cache hunting, and other forms of hunting, this detector type is NOT best suited for all forms of treasure hunting and prospecting.

However, some are designed with distinct, dual circuitry modes (one VLF universal and one automatic ground elimination mode) which enable them to perform all functions with top efficiency.

All detector types, of course, can be used more or less effectively in all forms of hunting, but for best results you should select the detector (and/or circuit mode) most suited for the type of hunting you are doing. Automatic ground elimination circuitry is simply not designed for, nor is it capable of, all purpose hunting without reduced efficiency.

CIRCUITRY

Automatic ground elimination circuitry is basically of the automatic sensing type that monitors the composition of the illuminated area beneath the searchcoil. (The illuminated area is primarily that area directly beneath the searchcoil which is penetrated by the searchcoil's electromagnetic field.) The circuitry operates automatically to take continuous and automatic readings on this illuminated area to determine the iron mineral content and adjust the circuitry to eliminate detection of the iron mineral.

Also, some of these detectors automatically keep the detector tuned to the pre-determined silent or threshold audio operating point.

Since the monitoring described above is automatic, the detector cannot be hovered (held stationary) over detected targets. If the searchcoil is held motionless, no detection signals will be generated. Consequently, slight searchcoil motion is always necessary. Certain models, of this type, however, can be scanned much more slowly than others.

ALL METAL/TARGET ELIMINATION MODES

In addition to features described above, Automatic Ground Elimination detectors are capable of both all-metal detection and target elimination. Most detectors of this type have an adjustable control that allows the operator to determine which trash or unwanted targets he or she wishes not to detect.

Some automatic elimination detectors also have dual channels, a feature which allows the operator to adjust the detector to classify targets with one or two detection "windows." For a complete description of detector "window," refer to the author's book, MODERN METAL DETECTORS. A detector window is a feature of some instruments that permits the operator to dial in on one or more target ranges or categories that can be either detected or not detected to suit the requirements of the operator. A conveniently mounted control allows the operator to switch between channels.

For instance, one channel may be adjusted to eliminate the detection of bottle caps while accepting coins (including nickels) and rings. The second channel may be adjusted to eliminate detection of pull tabs while accepting all silver and clad coins. The operator can scan along in the bottle cap rejection mode as the primary operating mode. When the target is detected, he can momentarily switch to the pull tab mode to determine if the object falls within the bottle cap and pull tab category. This procedure gives the operator a great deal of additional knowledge about detected targets.

Most Automatic Ground Elimination detectors can be operated either silently or at slight audio threshold level. There is little difference in the operating capabilities of either silent or threshold operation. Threshold operation gives a very slight edge on depth, such that when the detector is operated with slight threshold sound, targets lying in the outer recesses of the fringe area may be detected. Some fringe area detection will be lost in the silent mode, but this loss is very small, amounting only to about one or two percentage points.

Operation with slight threshold gives a small advantage in contouring detected targets. "Contouring" means the outlining or shape determination of detected targets. For all practical purposes, however, either silent or threshold audio operation is highly satisfactory. Some prefer one setting and some prefer another.

PINPOINTING

Because of the nature of the automatic detector type, pinpointing detected targets is more difficult than with other types of detectors. Many people find pinpointing very imprecise, at best.

Certain Automatic Ground Elimination detectors feature electronic pinpointing. While depressing a switch, that activates a special electronic circuit, the operator scans back over detected targets, thereby achieving a greatly improved pinpointing capability. Electronic pinpointing circuitry electronically "sharpens" the detection signal when the target is directly below the center of the searchcoil.

In effect, what is happening is that the detector electronic pinpointing mode activates a true non-automatic electronic gain control mode that achieves excellent pinpointing even when the searchcoil is hovered above the target.

Another feature of the electronic pinpointing mode is that the detector can be detuned or, in effect, tuned TO THE TARGET, thus achieving extremely precise pinpointing. This is achieved simply by hovering above the target, releasing and then pressing the electronic pinpointing switch. See your detector instruction manual for more details.

DETECTION DEPTH

The Automatic Ground Elimination detector type ranks extremely high in depth detection capability. Not only is it capable of reaching to great depths to detect coins, but its extremely sharp, fast response signal is unmistakable when coins and other objects are detected. The signals are much improved over the old TR "quick response" signal that in past years was so popular.

The detection depth capability of Automatic Ground Elimination detectors is equal to that of quality VLF and pulse detectors.

SEARCHCOILS

All types of searchcoils, including the co-planar, co-axial, concentric, and others, are used with about equal efficiency. No searchcoil type is perfect and all have both desirable and less desirable operating characteristics. The seven-to-eight-inch diameter searchcoils are preferred simply because they are lightweight, compared to larger types, and their size gives good depth and scanning width.

Even though all types can be constructed to be submersible, all are not so made, and it is best to check the individual manufacturer's specifications to learn whether his searchcoils are splashproof, waterproof, or submersible. There are definite differences among these categories.

It is often popularly believed that all searchcoils are electrostatically shielded. If they are not, they certainly should be. Electrostatic shielding prevents false signals from, for example, grass, weeds, ground, nearby nonmetallic objects, etc.

The dynamic range of all Automatic Ground Elimination detector searchcoils is very wide. Dynamic range means primarily the variation or range of target sizes that can be detected to acceptable depths by any one given searchcoil. For instance, a seven- or eight-inch searchcoil can detect objects as small as a BB and all targets up to the size of a battleship. As a comparison, eight-inch diameter BFO searchcoils may not be capable of detecting targets as small as BBs.

TIPS ON USING YOUR AUTOMATIC GROUND ELIMINATION DETECTOR

While the scope of this book is not meant to include full operating instructions for all types of detectors, basic operating characteristics and numerous tips are presented. The most important thing is to understand that you must learn how to use your detector regardless of its type. Failure to do so will result in ineffective performance and reduced success.

First, insist on training from the shop where you purchase your detector. This initial training step should not be overlooked. Before purchase, question the dealer about the type of training you will receive. If it does not seem adequate, perhaps you should seek another dealer from whom to buy.

This Automated VLF Ground Elimination detector, the Freedom 2, differs from the manually-adjustable VLF types in that the earth's mineralization is automatically eliminated from detection. The detector automatically and continuously evaluates the earth's mineral matrix beneath the search-coil and eliminates iron minerals from detection.

Read the instruction manual several times before beginning operation. If audio and video instruction cassettes are available, by all means obtain copies and play them numerous times, each time going through the various recommended procedures, controls, adjustments,and field operation tips with your detector. Memorize the names of the various controls, their functions, and how they are adjusted. As you go through this initial learning period, make every attempt to utilize your detector in the field and on your own test plot.

Even though manufacturers claim that the Automatic Ground Elimination instruments can be operated with equal success, either silently or with threshold audio, you should spend considerable time using your detector both ways to learn which you prefer. Not everyone has the same preference or hearing ability.

I recommend that you use your Automatic Ground Elimination detector with zero trash elimination (discrimination) for several hours and dig every target. This is the fastest, most complete way to learn the whole range of peculiarities and characteristics of your detector. As you gradually learn how to use the instrument, you can begin to dial in various levels of target elimination.

If optional searchcoils are available, study the characteristics of the various types and purchase those you believe would increase the effectiveness of your particular search efforts.

CHAPTER XIX

Understanding and Using BFO Detectors

BFO detectors are best classified as all-purpose instruments; they are capable of performing most all treasure hunting and prospecting tasks. In their day they excelled in all forms of hunting, but today's superior and varied equipment leaves only black magnetic sand hunting and ore sampling to be best accomplished by the peculiar capabilities of the BFO.

CAPABILITIES

BFO'S are only about fifty percent as effective as other detector types for coin hunting and all other treasure hunting tasks, including cache and relic hunting and prospecting. Various sizes of searchcoils are available to expand BFO capabilities.

CIRCUITRY

BFO circuitry cannot cancel iron earth minerals, nor can it cancel ocean beach salt. While a few tricks, so to speak, permit BFO operators to operate with good efficiency over highly mineralized ground, even though ground minerals cannot be eliminated 100-percent, these detectors cannot be as capable over-all as other types.

GROUND AND TARGET ELIMINATION

As just discussed, the BFO has no capability for eliminating or reducing the detection effects of earth minerals, but a few techniques can be used to help eliminate or reduce these effects: increasing the audio frequency to a slightly higher level, scanning with the searchcoil held at a higher than usual scanning height, and scanning the searchcoil at a faster than normal rate.

Some BFO's have a very good and accurate capability to eliminate trash targets from detection. This capability, however, is restricted to metered target identification while retaining correct audio metal/mineral target identification. The BFO always gives correct metal/mineral identification with 100-percent accuracy; that is, when adjusted to the metal tuning side of null, the detector will give a correct audio indication of the predominent element in ore samples, whether they be conductive metal or non-conductive iron mineral. This particular feature makes the BFO extremely valuable when prospecting. Detection of mag-

James R. Smith, Houston, Texas, has just located one of the gold pieces buried in this hunting field. Several gold pieces were buried in small glass bottles and became "finders', keepers'" if found by any of the contestants.

Johnny Kouba, Ennis, Texas, searches quickly for coins buried at a Houston THAP competition meet. Johnny and wife Kay are two of the best-known coin hunting professionals in the U.S.A.

netic black sand is excellent, especially when large searchcoils are used.

TUNING

BFO detectors can be audio tuned three ways: in the mineral, the metal, or the silent (in-between mineral and metal) mode.

When the detector is tuned to the mineral mode, conductive metal targets cause the frequency to decrease. Non-conductive iron mineral will cause the audio tone frequency to increase.

When the detector is set to the metal side of null, iron mineral causes the tone to decrease. Conductive metal targets cause the tone to increase in frequency.

When the detector is set to the null point, both non-conductive iron mineral and conductive metals cause the audio tone to increase in frequency. Remember that some sensitivity and depth detection are very definitely reduced when the detector is operated in the null zone.

167

PINPOINTING

There are no provisions for electronic pinpointing on BFO's, but normal pinpointing methods work very well. Pinpointing is very good with the BFO and the smaller the searchcoil, the more accurate the pinpointing that can be achieved. By reducing the tuning setting, perhaps even setting the tuning down in the null, pinpointing can be very sharp and precise.

COIN DEPTH

The BFO gives good coin depth, but it cannot achieve the detection depth possible with most other detector types

SEARCHCOILS

Many different BFO searchcoils are available, ranging in diameter size from three-quarter-inch to the very large 24x24-inch. There is a searchcoil to suit almost any type of BFO hunting. Most are very lightweight and highly maneuverable. All can be waterproofed and made submersible up to the connector. Electromagnetic shielding is very easy to achieve on BFO detector searchcoils. The dynamic range of BFO coils is not as wide as with other detector types.

Kenneth Wherry of Faulkton, SD, sent this photo of his friend, Merle Horning of Cresbard, SD. Merle systematically searches beaches, parks, and school yards. Among his many finds are 8 rings that he found in 3 hours of beach searching. One of the finds was a diamond ring. He searched among the populace of Cresbard until he found the owner who promptly awarded him a check for $175!

HOW TO USE YOUR BFO DETECTOR

To operate a BFO for coin hunting, it is best to use the six-inch diameter or perhaps even smaller searchcoils. BFO coils do not have the intense electromagnetic field of other types; consequently, the larger BFO searchcoils tend to be poor for coin hunting.

BFO's should be tuned to the metal side of null and set at an operating frequency of about 40-60 cycles per second. Since BFO's have no tuning push buttons or any kind of automatic tuning, it is best to lower the searchcoil to the operating height and then manually tune the detector to a 4060 cycle beat rate. Under non-mineralized conditions the searchcoil can be held close to the ground; however, the greater the degree of iron minerals the higher the searchcoil must be elevated. It should be held level and scanned in front of the operator at a rate of one to two feet per second. If ground minerals are extremely annoying, the scan rate can be increased considerably.

BFO SUMMARY

The BFO, while rated as the poorest and least used coin hunting detector, nevertheless has some excellent operating features which can be put to good use by the person who wants to achieve the best BFO results. As with any detector, the operator should read and study the manual and any other instructive material available and spend enough time in the field to become proficient with this detector type.

CHAPTER XX

Understanding and Using TR Detectors

TR (transmitter-receiver) detectors are like other types in that an electromagnetic field is transmitted by the searchcoil into the area surrounding the searchcoil. Metal objects that come within the area directly beneath the searchcoil create sufficient disturbance of the transmitted field so that targets are detected.

While TR's are not very popular today, over the many years of their greatest popularity multiple millions of coins were found. Today, generally speaking, TR's are manufactured only in lower cost models and are used in special applications.

CAPABILITIES

TR's have always been thought of and classified mainly as deep coin hunting detectors. They were never popular for cache hunting due to their inability to eliminate the detection of iron earth minerals. Their detection of and quick response to iron mineral makes them poor prospecting instruments.

GROUND/TARGET ELIMINATION

TR's cannot ignore or eliminate the detection effects of iron earth minerals, and salt detection can be eliminated only if the detector is equipped with an adjustable target elimination control. Most TR's have excellent target elimination circuitry. Some TR's have fully adjustable target elimination controls; others have switches with factory pre-set target elimination adjustments that give the operator limited, though useful target elimination selection.

TUNING

For maximum sensitivity and depth detection, TR's are best tuned to slight audio threshold. They can be operated silently, but it must be understood that silent operation does give reduced TR sensitivity and detection depth.

PINPOINTING

Pinpointing is easily accomplished with a TR since it has very sharp detection signal characteristics. Detected coins will cause precise, sharp, positive audio signals generally when they lie beneath the center of the searchcoil. No electronic pinpointing capabilities are available for TR's.

COIN DEPTH

TR's give good depth on coins, but it should be remembered that they cannot eliminate the effects of iron earth minerals and that detection depth in moderate to highly mineralized ground will be reduced.

SEARCHCOILS

TR searchcoils can be manufactured in a wide variety of sizes, but since TR's are not produced for the professional market, searchcoil size selection may be limited. The most popular size is the seven to eight-inch diameter which gives good depth and scanning width. TR searchcoils have a wide dynamic range and they can be produced in submersible models and with electrostatic shielding.

HOW TO USE YOUR TR DETECTOR

TR's should be used with headphones, as should all other detectors, and should be tuned to achieve a very faint audio threshold level for best sensitivity and operating depth. To operate TR's silently will reduce sensitivity and depth, but, since TR's cannot eliminate the effects of iron earth minerals, they may of necessity have to be operated in the silent region in highly mineralized areas. Because the TR responds to iron minerals, even very slight up and down movements of the searchcoil, holes in the ground, uneven places, or other anomalies of the search area may cause TR audio to be extremely erratic and necessitate the use of various operating "tricks" or special techniques. Two such procedures are to operate the detector silently and to place the searchcoil directly upon the ground and use a scrubbing motion so as to eliminate up and down motions of the coil.

CHAPTER XXI

Understanding and Using Pulse Induction Detectors

Pulse detectors are highly capable instruments generally used for beach, surf, and underwater hunting. They rate very high for coin hunting, especially when used on the beach or in ocean surf situations. In fact, because of their ability to ignore ocean beach salt and magnetic black sand, the pulse detector can be used over such ground conditions with the highest degree of efficiency.

Their bell-ringing audio response is slightly different from that of other types of detectors. It enhances the operator's ability to hear detection signals, especially in surf areas and when used by divers underwater.

The bell-like sound was produced initially so that it could be heard even when scuba equipment was worn. Such equipment, as you may know, provides divers with an air supply, and, when a diver breathes underwater, the resulting bubbles make noise which can interfere with the ability of the operator to hear detection signals. The bell-ringing pulse sound enhances the target detection signal so that the operator can hear it more readily.

Pulse detectors characteristically have more battery drain than other detector types and the extra weight of their battery packs makes them somewhat heavier than other instruments.

CAPABILITIES

Pulse detectors perform well in most cache hunting applications, but they are not recommended for prospecting. Even though most pulse detectors are designed primarily for beach hunting or underwater use, when larger searchcoils are available pulse detectors are capable of locating deep money caches. Pulse instruments can also be used on dry land in park areas with a quite acceptable degree of efficiency.

Since pulse detectors perform so admirably on salt water beaches that contain magnetic black sand, they are generally constructed with waterproof and/or submersible housings and searchcoils.

During the first few years after pulse instruments were introduced to the treasure hunter, they were generally very expensive and designed almost exclusively for underwater applications. Manufacturers have, however, now succeeded in producing covertible pulse detectors that can be used both on the beach and underwater.

Several treasure hunters, including Indian John, Joseph Pompey, and the author, search for Spanish coins at one of the well publicized Florida coastline shipwreck sites. Indian John relates how he found a cache of coins near here by working during a storm. The wind, wave, and rain actions move the sand around, and it was in a wash that he found the coins. These "washes" sometimes only last for a short time as the storm action sometimes fills them quickly. The motor and barge framework are all that are left of one of Mel Fisher's prop wash barges that was blown ashore during a storm.

The convertible feature and the very competitive prices currently offered have resulted in a great increase in the popularity of pulse detectors. They, certainly, are rated as Number One coin producers in ocean beach, highly magnetic black sand situations. (Note: Automatic Ground Elimination detectors that have adjustable target elimination modes can also be used succesfully on ocean beaches.) If the detector is to be used on the beach or in the water, it is best to use those manufactured with submersible control housings.

CIRCUITRY

Pulse circuitry is different from other types. All other detector types discussed in this book utilize what is termed "continuous wave operation." That is, they continuously transmit a signal. Pulse detectors, on the other hand, transmit intermittently; e.g.,they transmit a pulse of electromagnetic energy of short duration. Then, the searchcoil and circuits "wait" for return signals from the metal targets.

The burst of energy created when the searchcoil electromagnetic field is generated enters the ground and any metal targets that are illuminated by this electromagnetic field energy generate what is called a secondary electromagnetic energy field. This secondary field radiates in all directions, with a portion of it radiating back toward the searchcoil. Immediately after the initial transmission, all power is shut off and the instrument awaits the return of signals from detected targets. This system is very good and results in the capability ignoring about 90 percent iron earth minerals and salt minerals.

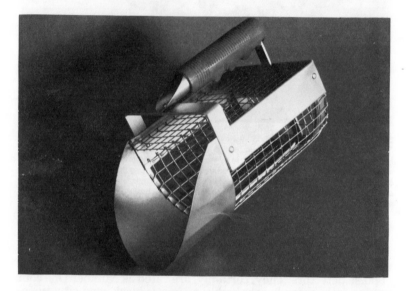

This sturdy coin scoop is one of the handiest tools a coin hunter can have for quick, sure retrieval of coins and jewelry from beaches and sandy areas. It greatly speeds up recovery of detected finds. For information, see your Garrett metal detector equipment dealer.

GROUND/TARGET ELIMINATION

As just stated, pulse detectors ignore iron earth and salt minerals, but in addition certain models of pulse instruments have target elimination modes which do a very good job of eliminating most unwanted targets, including pull tabs. Pulse detectors, however, do not do as good a job of eliminating iron nail detection as do other detector types.

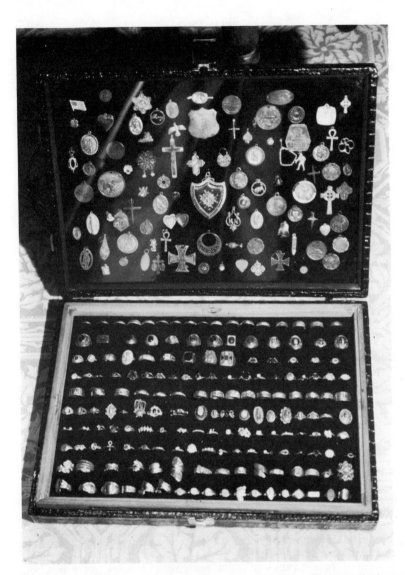

These rings and medallions are only a very tiny fraction of the vast beach treasures that have been found by T. R. Edds, P.O. Box 1133, Merritt Island, FL 32952. Mr. Edds has spent many, many years searching for treasure on Florida beaches with his good friend Walter Stark. These men have mastered the art of beachcombing with detectors. As proof they have amassed thousands upon thousands of coins, rings, jewelry, relics, and other objects during their searches.

TUNING
Pulse detectors should be tuned for faint threshold sound. Even though they can be operated silently, silent operation is not recommended because of loss of depth detection and sensitivity.

COIN DEPTH
Pulse detectors are highly capable of detecting coins, rings, and similar objects to extreme depths. When a pulse is used in some salt water environments, a depth multiplier effect takes place that causes it to give increased detection on coins.

Metal detectors must work perfectly under all conditions. Here, the author and his son spend time on a Texas beach testing and evaluating several different types of detector circuits and searchcoils. Metal detectors must be designed to operate perfectly in extremes of temperature, moisture and ground mineral conditions. A great amount of testing in various parts of the United States is required to insure that the above adverse conditions present no problems.

SEARCHCOILS
A wide range of searchcoils is available for pulse detectors. Those smaller in diameter than about three inches have very little practical application for the coin hunter. The most popular are the seven-to-ten-inch diameter sizes which give good detection and excellent scanning width. The larger the size, however, the poorer is the pinpointing.

Submersible searchcoils can be produced with very effective electromagnetic shielding.

The dynamic range of pulse searchcoils is very good, but not quite as good as automatic ground elimination and VLF searchcoil types.

While searchcoils can be manufactured in various diameter sizes, the most practical are from three inches up to about twelve inches or larger. The Smaller coils give excellent pinpointing results and can be maneuvered into small spaces. Twelve-inch and larger searchcoils give excellent depth on both small and large objects, but small object pinpointing is more difficult.

176

HOW TO USE YOUR PULSE DETECTOR

Pulse detectors are very easy to operate and use: simply turn the instrument on, adjust the audio to slight threshold, and start scanning. Iron earth minerals and salt water will not be detected. Only metallic objects will produce detection signals.

Searchcoils can be held very close to the ground but they usually have to be scanned at a slightly slower rate than other detector types because pulse instruments characteristically have a slower detection response.

Pinpointing is slightly more difficult than with, say, the VLF types, but it none the less is very acceptable, especially after a certain amount of practice.

All instructive material—manuals, audio and video tapes when available— should be utilized to the fullest, the same as when learning to operate any other detector type. Learn to use your pulse detector not only for coin hunting on the beach, in swimming areas, and in salt water—the applications for which it is especially recommended—but also for scanning land areas where performance will be very good.

CHAPTER XXII

Understanding and Using VLF Detectors

Until the development of the Automatic Ground Elimination detector type, the VLF had the coin hunting field mostly to itself was the preferred coin hunting detector. Quality VLF's are highly capable of performing all coin hunting, treasure hunting, and prospecting tasks. They detect very deeply and can be built with many desirable features.

The author tests one of the new VLF ground eliminating detectors near Cripple Creek, Colorado. The new VLF detector types allow the operator to balance out the adverse effects of mineralized ground completely, without reducing the detector's sensitivity. This new circuit technique actually greatly enhances sensitivity.

CAPABILITIES

Quality-built VLF instruments have been accepted as universal application detectors and can accomplish almost every task. They have an extremely wide range of capabilities, meeting not only all coin hunting requirements, but also cache and relic hunting, ghost-towning, and prospecting functions with great ease and

These items were found at one of Gen. Patton's desert training camps by Bob Grant and Bob Wolfe of Treasure Emporium, 6507 Lankershire Blvd., N. Hollywood, California 91606.

efficiency. A wide range of searchcoils adds to their popularity because the wider the range of available coils, of course, the more tasks the detectors can perform.

Since quality VLF detectors are so highly capable, they can be selected and used with the utmost confidence. If you are interested not only in coin hunting but also in other forms of hunting, this detector type is highly recommended as a valuable addition to your metal detecting equipment.

CIRCUITRY

VLF detectors utilize circuitry very similar to that of the TR in that instruments both transmit and receive, but the VLF goes several steps further because it can be built with manual controls to adjust out iron mineral detection.

Various other functions, such as target elimination, pinpointing, coin depth indication, etc., can be readily adapted to VLF circuitry. They are highly capable, extremely deeply detecting instruments from which, if they are quality built, the user can expect the highest degree of performance in all phases of coin hunting, general treasure hunting, and prospecting.

GROUND/TARGET ELIMINATION

From their introduction, VLF detector types have been capable of operating over highly iron mineralized ground. Highly efficient trash elimination modes can be adapted to the VLF, thus giving it high performance and efficiency in coin hunting applications. As will be described later, various special metered and audio target classification and elimination (discrimination) circuitry is available for these instruments, features which enhance VLF detector status as superb, high quality coin hunting instruments even more.

TUNING

Manually tuned VLF's are best operated with slight audio threshold sound. This tuning is generally accomplished with the manual rotation of a knob. VLF's can be operated silently, but depth detection and sensitivity will suffer somewhat and silent operation with a standard tuning VLF is not recommended.

PINPOINTING

While pinpointing characteristics of VLF detectors are very good, electronic pinpointing circuitry can be adapted to give the VLF operator even greatly ability to pinpoint detected targets. The electronic pinpointing feature is generally present in the form of an operating mode that is brought into play when a button is pushed while the searchcoil is scanned over the target.

Veteran treasure hunters Tommy T. Long of Outdoor Hobby Supply in Lewiston, Idaho, and Roy Lagal, also of Lewiston, recover coins from this heavily worked park. The new VLF type detectors penetrate so deeply that areas which have been worked countless times before are paying off handsomely in old coins buried too deeply for standard TR and BFO detectors. One coin hunter, after he had begun to use the new VLF types, remarked, "These new VLF's penetrate so deeply I am scared to dig any deeper!"

COIN DEPTH

Certainly, the VLF rates at the very top of detection depth capability and does not take a back seat to any other detector type when over-all performance is considered. Extreme depth can be achieved with a VLF in all phases of coin and treasure hunting and prospecting.

A special circuit called "coin depth measuring" is available on several models and brands of VLF detectors. The meter is calibrated for coin size targets only. Smaller and larger targets will produce somewhat erroneous coin depth measurement readings, but the fact that the depth of most coins can be determined very accurately gives the coin hunter desirable information about detected coins before they are dug.

SEARCHCOILS

Several different types and styles of searchcoils are available for VLF instruments, ranging in size from a three-quarter-inch diameter probe to twelve-, fourteen-, and sixteen-inch diameter searchcoils. VLF searchcoils have an extremely wide dynamic

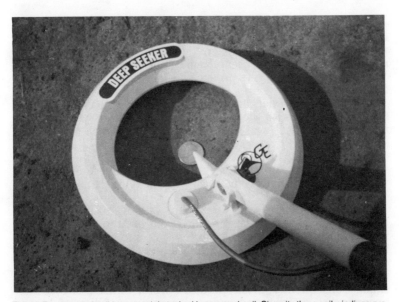

This VLF type searchcoil is a co-axial stacked loop searchcoil. Since its three coil windings are wound on spools, many problems encountered in the past with production of other type searchcoils have been overcome. This type of stacked loop construction eliminates 60-cycle power and other electromagnetic field disturbances. The searchcoil pattern allows quick pinpointing. TR discrimination "back reading" false signals, common to other searchcoils, are eliminated.

These coins are among many which have been found recently in Greece. The two coins on the left are from a total find of 25 coins that dated from the period 400 B.C. Mr. and Mrs. Charles Garrett have begun an effort to introduce detector instrumentation into the field of archaeology. Metal detectors are virtually unknown in Europe and, obviously, if detectors were utilized in the correct manner, countless thousands of priceless archaeological treasures could be discovered.

range, can be built to be submersible, and can be constructed with very efficient electromagnetic shielding. Even though just about any size and model searchcoil can be obtained for use with a VLF, some manufacturers produce a wider range of model choices than do others.

Co-planar, co-axial, and concentric searchcoil types are the most requested, with the seven-to-eight-inch diameter being the most popular. That size gives excellent coin depth and a wide scanning path.

Searchcoils of 10 ½-inch diameter have become very popular with coin hunters because they give extra, added depth and a wide scanning path. Of course, they are heavier than the smaller coils.

Some professional coin hunters use twelve-inch searchcoils, but generally those and larger searchcoils are thought of primarily as being for cache and relic hunting and prospecting. The larger the searchcoil, the greater the depth capability, but the difference in depth capability between a twelve- and a fourteen-inch coil or between a fourteen- and a sixteen-inch coil is very small. Consequently, most operators prefer to use a twelve-inch because the weight and reduced maneuverability of larger searchcoils make them less desirable.

Searchcoils that can be lowered fifty feet for underwater use are available for the VLF and are quite popular.

As I have said many times in SUCCESSFUL COIN HUNTING, metal detecting is not just an adult hobby. The young fellow from Long Island, New York, Peter Sexton, seen in the photo above and on the following page, proves that the younger ones can find their share too. Peter has become very adept with his VLF/TR. He travels with his parents, Roy and Pat Sexton, owners of Hobbies Unlimited in Long Island, as they go from Canada to Texas searching for treasure. The whole family is active in TH'ing and Peter has practically everything he ever found which, by the way, is quite an impressive amount of treasure. The Sextons traveled to Massachusetts to attend the third Search International Treasure Hunt and while on the trip, he added 980 coins to his collection, a number of which are quite valuable. It doesn't matter whether the ground is heavily mineralized, Peter has learned how to use his detector and he can make it talk the money language.

SUPER-SNIPING

"Super-sniping" is searching for coins in high trash and so-called "worked out" areas with the aid of three-to-four-inch diameter searchcoils which produce a particularly intensive electromagnetic field over a small area.

When target elimination (discrimination) is used, good targets (such as coins) produce a positive audio signal. Trash or eliminated targets produce a negative or reduced volume signal. When two targets, one trash and one good, are detected at the same time, the signals tend to cancel one another. Consequently, when trash targets are in an area where coins are being hunted,

Here again is Peter Sexton (see preceding page) with just a few of his impressive collections of coins, rings, battlefield relics, and miscellaneous finds. While Peter's favorite hobby is coin hunting, he has also learned to use his detector for relic and battlefield hunting and has come up with some mighty good finds! Good hunting to you, Peter . . . don't let up!

many coin targets will be missed. The larger the searchcoil diameter, the greater the problem because more targets can be beneath the searchcoil at the same time.

The small diameter searchcoil with a high electromagnetic field intensity can be brought into play for "super-sniping." These especially designed searchcoils generate an extremely intense narrow electromagnetic field that shoots straight down into the ground past trash objects to detect individual coins. The result is that coins missed with other detectors can be readily detected.

DEPTH MULTIPLIER

The Bloodhound Depth Multiplier shown in the accompanying photograph, is a unique patented searchcoil, developed for use by cache hunters. This two-box searchcoil lives up to its name in that it greatly multiplies the depth capabilities of VLF detectors and is capable of detecting large metallic objects to depths of fifteen or twenty feet. It will not detect water, tree roots, or ground minerals, nor will it detect small pieces of metal, a characteristic especially valuable when searching around farm houses where nails and other small pieces of metallic trash abound. It will detect only the larger, deeply buried caches, coins, and similar targets.

HOW TO USE THE VLF DETECTOR

The VLF is very easy to use. For best results, adjust the audio for faint threshold sound. Silent operation of this detector in the manual VLF mode is not recommended as some depth will be lost.

If iron minerals are present in the soil, it may be necessary to adjust the ground elimination control in order to eliminate the detection effect of minerals. Operation on salt water beaches and in salt water is achieved by operating the instrument in the trash elimination mode. A point will be found near bottle cap elimination where salt water is not detected.

The searchcoil is best operated at one to two inches above the ground. It is a good idea to check, occasionally, for ground minerals by raising and lowering the searchcoil. If ground mineral content has changed since you last made an adjustment for it, the detector will give a slight audio indication meaning you should make a minor adjustment to the ground elimination control.

Scan the detector searchcoil the same as other searchcoils, at a rate of about one-to-two-feet per second in a straight line in front of you.

Because of the wide range of VLF capabilities and the fact it has various features not found on some other detectors, we particularly stress that you study the instruction manual and use audio and video instruction tapes where available in order to master and take full advantage of these truly outstanding detectors.

185

CHAPTER XXIII

Metal Trash Elimination and Target Classification

If your detector is a pre-1983 land model or a pre-1981 beach/underwater model, in all probability it features a basic discrimination circuit with an adjustable or selectable discrimination control whereby the operator can increase discrimination to reject more metal targets or decrease discrimination to accept more detected targets.

Today's more advanced detectors either ELIMINATE the detection of iron earth minerals, certain trash metal targets, etc., and/or they CLASSIFY certain detected minerals and targets into meaningful categories.

TERMINOLOGY

For years, the word "discrimination" designated a detector's capability to identify detected targets and alert the operator by audio and/or meter. Detectors featured a discriminating circuit that classified detected targets into two groups: "good" or "bad." Depending upon the amount of discrimination dialed in by the operator, the detector produced an audio volume decrease for rejected ("bad") targets and an audio volume increase for accepted ("good") targets and/or the meter deflected down ("bad") or up ("good).

Now that detector technology has advanced in its capability to supply the operator with greater target identification intelligence, "descrimination" is no longer appropriate to describe the junction of target identification circuitry. "Elimination and "classification" are the terms now being used to describe new, smarter detector circuit functions. It far more accurately describes what is taking place within a detector, not only in the target elimination mode but also in the ground identification mode.

TARGET CONDUCTIVITY IS THE KEY

The conductivity rating of any given metal (target) is a measure of how well it will conduct electricity. The national Bureau of Standards in Washington, DC, has established conductivity ratings for all known metals. Gold, silver, and copper have much higher conductivity ratings than does iron.

This is important to the metal detector operator because metal detectors can measure the conductivity of a detected target and compare it to a reference point.

METAL TRASH ELIMINATION

By means of the trash elimination control, the operator can select a conductivity point which tells the detector circuitry the dividing point between the higher conductivity metals the operator wishes to dig and the lower conductivity metals the operator does not wish to dig. The detector provides the operator with the desired knowledge by an automatically gives a speaker and/or meter, thus providing the operator with the desired knowledge. In other words, the detector tells the operator which detected objects should be dug and which should not, depending upon the operator's wishes.

The accompanying chart borrowed from my book, MODERN METAL DETECTORS, categorizes most of the metal targets an operator is likely to encounter. Targets are named on the chart according to their relative conductivity.

If the trash elimination pointer is placed arbitrarily at BOTTLE CAPS, all metal targets which are positioned to the left of the pointer are eliminated from detection; all targets which are positioned to the right of the pointer are detected.

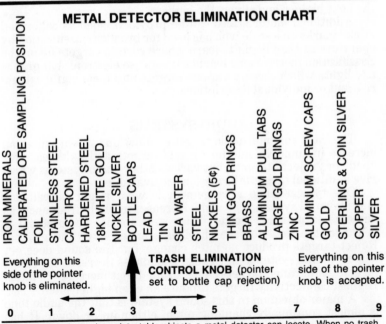

METAL DETECTOR ELIMINATION CHART

This chart lists the various detectable objects a metal detector can locate. When no trash elimination is dialed in (zero setting), all targets are detected. When the knob is set anywhere along the zero-to-nine scale, all objects toward lower numbers will be eliminated; all objects toward higher numbers will be accepted. NOTE: THIS CHART IS GENERAL AND ACTUAL RESULTS DEPEND UPON THE TYPE DETECTOR, DETECTOR FREQUENCY, ALLOYS, ETC., DETECTED. CONSEQUENTLY, YOU SHOULD MAKE YOUR OWN CHART USING YOUR OWN DETECTOR.

CLASSIFICATION

Beginning in the early '80s, some detectors became more sophisticated in that they could classify detected targets into meaningful categories. They could measure the specific conductivity of each detected target and produce an audio and/or meter response that classified or identified the targets more accurately. Thus, rather than a simple "yes" or "no," "good" or "bad" signal, as with earlier models, the operator was supplied with more than two conductivity categories.

TARGET CLASSIFICATION METERS

Meters or visual indicators have also become more sophisticated in that now some detectors have meters that identify individual targets. For example, a U.S.A. one-cent coin will read 1¢ on the meter. (Some meters even identify a penny as to whether it is copper or zinc.) A dime will read 10¢ on the meter; a quarter, 25¢, etc.

These target classification meters are further divided into at least three categories, the more popular being iron, gold, and silver. Iron represents objects with the lowest conductivity; gold, the next higher; and silver, the highest.

Additional meter scales can be provided, such as calibrated "tick" marks on a scale which is used for broader classification by operators as they begin to learn where certain targets lie on the classification meter. Some manufacturers use electronic bar graphs and lights which classify various targets into meaningful categories and/or individual descriptions.

AUDIO SYSTEMS

The most common audio target elimination system causes an increase in audio volume for "good" targets and a decrease for "bad" or "reject" targets, but various other audio systems which give additional target information are available.

One typical audio arrangement is what might be called a multi-layered system. The audio increases in pitch (frequency) as detected targets get better. That is, a normal audio sound is heard as the detector searchcoil is scanned over the ground. Reject targets produce no pitch change, but the sound does get louder. (Some systems may cause a loudness decrease for reject targets.) Mid-range targets cause a sound that increases in pitch. Highest conductivity targets produce an even higher pitch.

A major objection to this sound system is that the audio tone is almost continually changing pitch, either up or down. It has been described as akin to the sound of an early-day Ford Model A horn — Ahhhhhhhhh......Oooooooooooo......Gaaaaaaaaa!

A more effective system is one that is still multi-layered, but of a different character. Reject targets that are eliminated from detection cause the audio to decrease in volume. Mid-range targets cause the audio to increase in volume. Coins (highest conductivity) also cause the audio to increase in volume, but, in addition, a different audio tone is produced. This system requires no learning time for the operator to be able to decide which sound level the speaker produced and what it means in terms of target identification. There is far less guessing what the detector is trying to say.

GENERAL OBSERVATIONS

While the latest eliminator and target classification circuitry has become extremely accurate and quite acceptable, errors can creep in when, for example, targets lie at odd angles in the ground, when near by targets cause wrong readings, when metal targets contain alloys, etc.

In addition, there are many different kinds of pull tabs, some of which cause different readings. Iron bottle caps can cause different readings, also, depending upon how rusty they are and how they lie in the ground.

Nevertheless, in spite of the possibility for error, the efficiency and accuracy of the new elimination circuits and target classification indicators are very good and add a great deal to the enjoyment and success of detector operation.

Operators who use these latest detectors have learned that great value does come from the new elimination and target identification systems. With the tone alert classification system, an operator can set the detector to detect all targets, but the meter and/or audio tone tells the operator the nature of the target. With a quick flip of a switch, coin depth can be measured to give the operator a great amount of intelligence about each detected target. Some operators have become so proficient with the new instruments that they can literally read what is in the ground before they dig it.

Another consideration in favor of the tonal system is that unlighted target classification indicators cannot be seen at night. Also, glancing at a meter each time a target is detected often becomes tiring. An audio tone facilitates target identification and eliminates a certain amount of operator effort.

Smarter detectors are here to stay and engineering improvements will continue to make them smarter. Now is the time to trade in old equipment and get on the band wagon to enjoy the fruits of the metal detector engineer's labors!

CHAPTER XXIV

How to Care for Your Detector

Broadly speaking, the electronic circuitry in a metal detector is similar to that found in radios and high fidelity equipment, but the control housing is generally built more ruggedly because a metal detector is subjected to far more abuse than is a radio or any type of home entertainment electronics equipment. The detector is usually thrown in the back seat or the trunk of a car. It gets banged around, kicked, laid on the ground, bumped against trees, stumps, sidewalks, posts — you name it. It is operated in the rain, snow, dust storms, on the beach; it is submerged in water up to its neck. And, even cursed a little bit! By all rights, anything given this kind of treatment should ultimately require some kind of maintenance upkeep. However, most detectors are built solidly (or at least they should be) and can take it.

REASONABLE CARE

If you give your instrument reasonable care it should usually give you three to five years of uninterrupted service, barring catastrophic failure of transistors or other components. *First of all*, read the manufacturer's instruction manual. *Don't* wait until something has happened to your detector before you read the book. If there are things recommended for you to do by all means do them. Never purposely abuse your detector or subject it to damaging elements any more than you absolutely have to. Periodically check the batteries, and when they read at a low point replace them. Batteries in a run-down condition will leak, and almost overnight the acid could destroy some of the innards of your detector. Keep it as clean as possible, and occasionally open all battery doors, *etc.*, to remove all dust, dirt and lint with a slightly dampened rag. It is not a good idea to blow into it because dust and dirt could be blown into the controls. Keep all nuts, bolts and screws tight, and periodically check all coil cables for fraying and all connectors for tightness. If you have a carrying case, by all means use it for storage protection.

USE IT

On the other hand, don't baby your instrument simply for the sake of keeping it in sparkling new condition. Get out there and use that detector. Treat it as roughly as you must to do the best job you can in coin hunting. Quality detectors can take it, and your reward will be much greater. If you are not going to utilize your detector to its fullest capability, why buy it in the first place?

IF YOUR DETECTOR DOESN'T WORK

In the event your instrument should require maintenance, and time permits, write the manufacturer, explaining the trouble. There is always a possibility that the problem could be corrected without your having to send the instrument to the repair shop. For instance, if it works correctly on all search coils except one, in all probability that one search coil is all that should be returned to the factory. Sometimes peculiar operating characteristics are quite familiar to detector repairmen, and occasionally they can diagnose a problem by mail and correct it for the owner with much saving of time and money. *Always* check your batteries. If you suspect a problem check your instrument with batteries you know to be fresh. Visually inspect the instrument for loose nuts, bolts, wiring and other things. Sometimes just a loose screw holding a printed circuit board can cause an extremely erratic output.

SERVICE

If you must send your instrument to the factory follow this three-step method. Write a *brief* but complete failure analysis of the detector. Describe its trouble the best you can, but use as few words as possible. Your letter should be taped to the control housing so it is not lost in the packaging. Secondly, wrap the instrument as nearly like it was packaged when you received it new from the manufacturer. If the same type of material is not available, secure a strong cardboard box and pack several wadded up newspapers very tightly all around your instrument. If foam padding, bubble wrap or other type of packing material is available, by all means wrap this around the control housing and search coil before inserting them into the shipping box. After you have secured the instrument snugly inside the box tape the box securely with two-inch wide tape, followed with at least two to four strong cords wrapped around it. Thirdly, when you mail it back to the factory, follow the manufacturer's recommended procedure. If he says ship it *via* parcel post to his post office box, follow those instructions to the letter. It is little things like this which insure a more prompt turn-around of your repaired detector. If you need your instrument back by a certain date, do not hesitate to tell the manufacturer in the letter you enclose with the detector. You must, however, allow sufficient time for the manufacturer to receive the instrument, repair it, and then time for its return trip to you. If you need your instrument quickly, it is advisable to authorize the manufacturer to return the instrument to you air parcel post, collect for freight. Air Parcel Post charges run anywhere from $5 to $10.

It is surprising how few detectors of the total number sold must be returned to the factory for repair. So make every effort to care for your detector, and perhaps it will perform perfectly for you until the day you give it its long-deserved and well-earned rest.

New, advanced concepts such as audio and visual target classification, electronic pinpointing, coin depth measuring, and design for universal application are providing treasure, coin and relic hunters, as well as electronic prospectors, with capabilities only recently possible. Electronic components not previously available now allow design engineers to produce detectors that make all prior detector design concepts obsolete. This model, the Master Hunter 7 A.D.S., incorporates advanced circuit designs and state-of-the-art components. Target analyzers have reached such a high level of accuracy that some users believe near 95-percent identification is possible. The latest-design meter can classify all targets into meaningful categories and coins can be identified correctly before being dug. A unique audio system designed into this Master Hunter 7 A.D.S. accurately recognizes coins, regardless of their attitude in the ground. Even coins standing on edge will be correctly recognized. The operator hears a special bell-like tone when coins are detected. Bottle caps, pull tabs, screw caps, and other junk items do not produce the bell-like sound. This audio system tremendously increases the coin hunter's speed and efficiency.

CHAPTER XXV

A Few More Things You Will Need
to Know About Metal Detecting

HOLE IN YOUR POCKET WILL DO IT

It's difficult to understand why people will spend their hard-earned money purchasing a detector and then not take the time to learn to use it correctly. You must learn how to use your instrument in order to achieve the best results. If you are going to spend any time coin hunting why not do it as efficiently as possible? Read the instruction manual that comes with your instrument, not only once but several times. Practice with your instrument according to the instructions, and then get out in the field and get busy. Throughout this book you will find many tips to help you become more efficient and effective with your detector. Learn these different tips and techniques; practice them. Try to understand fully all there is to know and learn about your instrument. Read several good metal detector books.

Of course, if you are still reluctant to make the effort that you should you can still find coins if you follow this advice given by "Pinky" Nobel: "Cut a hole in your pocket, put some coins in your pocket, and follow yourself around. You'll find lots of coins."

HOW TO SCAN WITH YOUR DETECTOR

To scan with your detector it is best to let the coil overlap slightly with each sweep. If you are searching with a BFO or a Total Response (wide or total scan) detector it is advisable to overlap approximately 25%. In other words, after you make each sweep with, say, an eight-inch-diameter search coil, on the next sweep you should not move the search coil ahead the full eight inches but only approximately six inches. This will give the overlapping required to insure you are completely covering a given area. In using narrow scan TR's you should move your search coil ahead only approximately two to three inches on each sweep.

How rapidly should you scan with your detector? It is a mistake to scan with your search coil at too slow a speed, just as it is to scan at too fast a speed. The inexperienced operator should begin at a scanning rate of approximately one foot/second, whether using a TR or BFO. After a few hours practice the operator can begin to increase his speed up to a maximum of approximately two feet/second. Only the most skilled operators should scan faster than two feet/second. You should work toward increasing your scanning speed, however, because you will be able to cover large areas more quickly and greatly increase your take.

COIL "SWINGING" IMPORTANT

Probably the majority of detector operators swing their search loop in front of them in an arc. A few operators move their search coils in front of them in a straight line. I prefer the straight line method. Roy Lagal of Lewiston, Idaho, first demonstrated this straight line method to me many years ago. In my opinion it is far superior to the arc method for several reasons. A much wider path can be covered in a single scan; the coil can be held at a more even height throughout the full scan; the operator can cover the ground more efficiently without skipping. The straight line method gives the best exercise. If you have not yet tried the straight line method . . . give it a try. It may seem awkward at first, but you will soon get the "swing" of it.

Swing the search coil from side to side in front of you in a straight line. If you make sweeps wider than approximately four feet it will be necessary for you at the end of each sweep to twist slightly or rotate your body at the hips. Your feet will have to be approximately eighteen inches to

This straight line, side-to-side sweep is the best scanning method to use. More ground can be covered, and the coil can be kept at a constant height above the ground throughout the full sweep.

two feet apart in order to make the extra wide sweeps. As you approach the end of each sweep you will see how easy it is to keep your search coil at a given height above the ground. If you practice this method and work up a good rhythm I believe you will actually *enjoy* this "exercise."

SUPER SNIPING FOR COINS

Today, many detector users are going from larger searchcoils to smaller ones to find more coins.

With the advent of such coils as Garrett Electronics' 3½-inch Super-Sniper, coin hunters are learning the value of small coils in searching tight, narrow locations that won't accept larger searchcoils and in areas of high trash concentration.

The co-axial version of these smaller searchcoils can be worked right on top of both iron and aluminum trash and still produce hot detection signals on coins.

Because of their small size, these coils tend to ignore most ground mineralization, a common factor in masking signal strength when detectors are used in the discrimination mode. They also eliminate the backreading sounds from items being rejected and can be worked extremely close to metal posts and fences without producing signals.

While Garrett's Super-Sniper was produced as a nugget locating coil — and it works well for that purpose — most persons are using it primarily for coin hunting. Jerry Pattee, a Massachusetts coin hunter, found 118 coins along and around the foundations of a destroyed apartment complex. "The coil's small size, its powerful, highly concentrated signal, and its totally negative backreading were the main factors in making these finds," he says.

Users of these coils have to learn to work more slowly and methodically and to expect less depth of detection capability.

The secret is getting out, and thousands of coins that are hidden in trash or tucked into tight spots are being found. One of these small coin hunting wonders makes a welcome addition to any coin hunter's arsenal of metal detecting accessories.

METAL POSTS, ETC.

It is difficult to search along fence rows or adjacent to buildings which have metal sidings; in parks or playgrounds up close to the tumble gyms, slides, and swings; or adjacent to parking meter metal posts. The metal in these objects prevents the operator from scanning up close, unless the operator knows how to null them out. This is quite easily done.

You should search with your detector as you normally would until your detector begins to respond to the nearby metal object. When this occurs, there are two things you can do. If you are along a fence or searching adjacent to a metal building you can scan with your coil held as parallel as possible to the metallic object. This will give a uniform detector response and will allow you, with practice, to search normally. However, even this method does not work when you are quite close to the metallic object. The best way to search under these conditions is to place the detector against the metallic object as closely as you wish to search. Adjust the instrument *barely* down into the null or quiet region. Then scan holding the coils as nearly parallel to the metallic object as possible. This procedure will reduce sensitivity to buried objects, but at least it will allow you to search to some degree for possible coins in these areas. Since few treasure hunters have mastered this technique or know anything about it, you must employ it. It may result in a real bonanza!

NOTHING!

This is a common complaint. Recently I had a telephone call from a treasure hunter who told me he was searching under an old tree and got a faint indication on his detector. He began to dig, and dug deeper and deeper. Each time he stopped digging and scanned the hole with his detector he got an even louder indication. This prompted him to dig deeper and deeper until finally he had dug so deeply he had exposed the tap root and most of the other tree roots. He said he could look up while standing in the hole and see the main part of the tap root. He asked me what he should do. I told him to get out of the hole! This is a good example of a person who did not know what to expect of his instrument and had not learned to use it correctly.

FALSE (?) INDICATIONS

One might say, "I thought metal detectors did not give false signals . . . that they gave indications only on metal targets and some mineral targets." It is true that detectors with 100% electrostatically-shielded (top and bottom) search coils do not give false indications. For every indication that is not a metal or mineral target the apparent mis-indication is due either to poor design as explained under the detection section on Faraday-shielded coils or is a result of operator inadequacies. "False" holes, however, are there to be found, and you may detect one or more of them each time you use your detector. "False" holes are caused by several things.

ON END

Occasionally a person may think he has dug a false hole. However, this may not be the case. When coin hunting you can sometimes cut a plug, remove the plug, and check it with your detector and get no reading. You scan over the hole and do not get a reading. Thus you wonder what is wrong. Coins have been known to become dislodged from their flat position in the ground only to fall further down into the hole and land on end in a vertical position. As you know, a deeply buried coin standing on end is very difficult to detect. So even though you think there is nothing in the hole dig out a litle more dirt and sift the dirt through your fingers.

MAGNETS

Often a detector signal will be heard, and the operator will dig and find nothing. This can sometimes be caused by rusty objects such as tin cans or bottlecaps. It is a good idea to purchase a small, powerful magnet to carry with you. When you rub the magnet into the dirt, any iron that is there will become attached to the magnet, and you can see it. And the mystery of another false hole is solved!

FOIL

A detector may give a metallic response on a small bit of foil or a gum wrapper. The operator begins to dig; the small bit of foil crumples or is rolled up into a small ball and cannot be detected when the operator scans the loose dirt or the hole with his detector. The operator is perplexed; what is wrong? The instrument gave a reading, but no metallic object was located.

Care should be exercised in the exact pinpointing of all detector responses. Small bits of foil generally produce a high squeal on a detector, and if your instrument is not a discriminator you must decide the target is a piece of foil and not bother with it, or carefully lift out the first one or two inches of soil and inspect it for the foil or other tiny object. Another small object which produces a large response is a .22 shell. After these shells have been exposed to the ground for a year or longer they produce a very large signal. Because of their size and color they are often overlooked by the detector operator after they are dug up. Thus the operator may continue digging a deeper and deeper "false" hole.

IRON MINERALIZATION

Again, as the operator scans his detector across a hole, he gets a positive indication. He will dig a little deeper, scan with his detector again, receive another metallic response, and continue digging until soon he has a monstrous, gaping hole. You may ask, "Why does a detector

197

give a metal indication over a hole?" It gives a metal indication over some holes the same as it will give a metal indication over flat ground. The explanation for this is somewhat complex, but with a little careful study it is quite easily understood.

As we have noted, most ground contains some mineralized negative-reaction iron. If the detector search coil is lowered to the ground it drives the oscillator in the negative or mineral direction. In order for the operator to search correctly over this type ground the tuning knob must be turned to adjust the oscillator more into the positive or metal region. This positive adjustment cancels the negative reaction caused by the ground. In this way the detector's circuitry is manually adjusted *positive*. As the operator scans across the ground the detector continues to cancel out the negative ground. If, however, the coil is passed over a place in the ground where the negative-reacting iron has been removed or neutralized the detector will produce a positive indication because the ground negative disturbing force was removed, allowing the positive electronic adjustment to sound off through the speaker.

ABSENCE AND SALT

Spots of ground which have an absence or a low concentration of mineral can be caused in several different ways. A hole could be dug for a post, and in later years the post might be removed and the hole filled with non-mineralized ground. A wash can cause this problem. Also, a fire can create the same effect. In grounds which have conductive salts metal detectors will react positively to the salt. The wetter the ground, the greater will be the positive indication. In an area that is predominantly positive, yet which contains very little moisture, the ground will appear as neutral. However, if there is a shallow place or a sink hole that can contain moisture the moisture will cause the salts to become conductive, and as the detector is passed over this area a positive indication is produced.

With practice an operator can learn to determine quite accurately whether his detector response is due to a metal target or a false hole. Continue with me; it is not difficult to understand.

SMALL COIL'S DEPTH

When you are searching with your detector and receive a positive signal, scan the spot with the smallest coil available. If your instrument is a BFO and is equipped with independently operated dual search coils the job is much easier. If you become familiar with each detector search coil and know the maximum depth capability of each search coil, you will know the maximum depth to which your search coils will penetrate. Thus, as you pass over a spot with your smallest coil and get a positive indication, you will know approximately the maximum depth the target can be. As you begin to dig or probe you can stop when you have reached the depth to which you are confident the small coil can reach.

PROBES

There are other methods that can be used to determine if you have metallic objects or a false hole. You can use a two or three foot probe rod of approximately ¼″-⅜″ diameter. Military rifle cleaning rods are good for this purpose or, if you wish you can make a probe. I know treasure and cache hunters who probe the ground every time before they dig any hole. They have become quite adept at this, and can tell you if they have struck a rock, a tin can, glass, wood, or even if they encounter different types of soil layers. When a probe touches a buried object, it produces a reaction or vibration peculiar to the type of object. The vibra-

"Hardrock" Hendricks searches for coins and artifacts. He found several valuables, the best of which was a gold coin.

tions are transmitted up the handle and into the hands of the operator. It is best to use a metal handle welded securely to your test probe.

CONTOURING

Another method for determining if you have a false hole is to scoop out the ground in a bowl-shaped manner, the diameter of which is at least three times the diameter of the smallest coil you have available. After you have done this, scan with the coil in the hole, carefully following the contour of the hole. In that way the search coil will remain an equal distance from the ground or the bottom of the hole whether it be on the side or on the bottom. Generally, the detector will not give other than the same response over all areas of the "false" hole.

For your own benefit you should master the techniques described. Once learned, they could save you hours of needless digging.

TREASURE HUNTERS' CLUBS

I think it fitting that the last paragraph in SUCCESS-FUL COIN HUNTING be devoted to treasure hunters' clubs. There are approximately four hundred clubs in the United States and other countries. Members are treasure hunters just like you and me who have found a great hobby and enjoy the rewards that come from participating in the activity. Most TH'ers are members of one or more groups because we have learned that from such associations of fellow TH'ers come benefits that not only help us to be more successful but also help keep our hobby strong and protect it from damaging legislation. I encourage you to join your local club and Search International. Search is an active, world-wide organization of amateur and professional treasure hunters who are united in a determined and coordinated effort to promote, preserve, and protect the hobby of treasure hunting. Through Search periodicals, treasure hunts, and public seminars, treasure hunters are kept abreast of the latest treasure hunting and club news and events, as well as current information about equipment, hunting techniques, legislation which might affect the treasure hunter, and related subjects of which the treasure hunter should be aware. To join and begin receiving their publication, THE SEARCHER, send your name, address, and $3 for one year's dues to Search, P.O. Box 473007, Garland, Texas 75047.

This extremely rare gold coin is one of my most prized possessions. It was given to me by a friend who found the coin in Europe. It was minted approximately 40-20 B.C. and was in circulation during the time of Christ! Isn't it fantastic how a metal detector can, quite suddenly, span a gap of 2000 years! The joy of treasure hunting . . . you never know what you'll dig up next!

AUTHOR'S CONCLUDING COMMENT

No final chapter to this book can be written. Detector operator expertise and detector instrumentation are both changing at a fantastic rate. Practice brings improved detector operator skills and tomorrow will bring advancements in metal detector designs. New places to search will be found; new detector applications will be discovered. This book is only a beginning . . . .

My desire has been to steer you down the road of SUCCESSFUL COIN HUNTING. Within its pages I have discussed the majority of what is presently known about the coin hunting hobby. Use this information to your best advantage, and, as my good friend Roy Lagal once remarked, ". . . ride out the rest of the trail and enjoy it!"

God bless you all . . . .

Charles Garrett

RECOMMENDED SUPPLEMENTARY BOOKS

The books described below are among the most popular books in print related to treasure hunting. If you desire to increase your skills in various aspects of treasure hunting, consider adding these volumes to your library.

MODERN METAL DETECTORS. Charles Garrett. Ram Publishing Company. NEW! This advanced handbook explains simply yet fully how to succeeed with your metal detector. Written for home, field, and classroom study, MMD provides the expertise you need for success in any metal detecting situation, hobby or professional. Easily understood chapters on specifications, components, capabilities, selecting and operating a detector, choosing searchcoils and accessories, and more — increase your understanding of the fascinating, rewarding fields of metal detector use. 544 pages. 56 Illustrations, 150 photos.

DETECTOR OWNER'S FIELD MANUAL. Roy Lagal. Ram Publishing Company. Nowhere else will you find the detector operating instructions that Mr. Lagal has put into this book. He shows in detail how to treasure hunt, cache hunt, prospect, search for nuggets, black sand deposits ... in short, how to use your detector exactly as it should be used. Covers completely BFO-TR-VLF/TR types, P.I.'s, P.R.G.'s, P.I.P.'s, etc. Explains precious metals, minerals, ground conditions, and gives proof that treasure exists because it has been found and that more exists that you can find! Fully illustrated. 236 pages.

ELECTRONIC PROSPECTING. Charles Garrett, Bob Grant, Roy Lagal. Ram Publishing Company. A tremendous upswing in electronic prospecting for gold and other precious metals has recently occurred. High gold prices and unlimited capabilities of VLF/TR metal detectors have led to many fantastic discoveries. Gold is there to be found. If you have the desire to search for it and want to be successful, then this book will show you how to select (and use) from the many brands of VLF/TR's those that are correctly calibrated to produce accurate metal vs. mineral identification which is so vitally necessary in prospecting. Illustrated. 96 pages.

GOLD PANNING IS EASY. Roy Lagal. Ram Publishing Company. Roy Lagal proves it! He doesn't introduce a new method; he removes confusion surrounding old established methods. A refreshing NEW LOOK guaranteed to produce results with the "Gravity Trap" or any other pan. Special metal detector instructions that show you how to nugget shoot, find gold and silver veins, and check ore samples for precious metal. This HOW, WHERE and WHEN gold panning book is a must for everyone, beginner or professional! Fully illustrated. 112 pages.

THE COMPLETE VLF-TR METAL DETECTOR HANDBOOK (All About Ground Canceling Metal Detectors). Roy Lagal, Charles Garrett. Ram Publishing Company. The unparalleled capabilities of VLF/TR Ground Canceling metal detectors have made them the number one choice of treasure hunters and prospectors. From History, Theory, and Development to Coin, Cache, and Relic Hunting, as well as Prospecting, the authors have explained in detail the capabilities of VLF/TR detectors and how they are used. Learn the new ground canceling detectors for the greatest possible success. Illustrated. 200 pages.

ROBERT MARX: QUEST FOR TREASURE. R. F. Marx. Ram Publishing Company. The true story of the discovery and salvage of the Spanish treasure galleon, *Nuestra Señora de la Maravilla*, lost at sea, January 1656. She went to the bottom bearing millions in gold, silver and precious gems. Be there with the divers as they find coins and priceless artifacts over three centuries old. Join Marx's exciting adventure of underwater treasures found. The story of the *flotas*, dangers of life at sea, incredible finds ... all are there. Over 50 photos. 286 pages

TREASURE HUNTER'S MANUAL #6. Karl von Mueller. Ram Publishing Company. The original material in this book was written for the professional treasure hunter. Hundreds of copies were paid for in advance by professionals who knew the value of Karl's writing and wanted no delays in receiving their copies. The THM #6 completely describes full-time treasure hunting and explains the mysteries surrounding this intriguing and rewarding field of endeavor. You'll read this fascinating book several times. Each time you will discover you have gained greater in-depth knowledge. Thousands of ideas, tips, and other valuable information. Illustrated. 318 pages.

TREASURE HUNTER'S MANUAL #7. Karl von Mueller. Ram Publishing Company. The classic! The most complete, up-to-date guide to America's fastest growing activity, written by the old master of treasure hunting. This is *the* book that fully describes professional methods of RESEARCH, RECOVERY, and TREASURE DISPOSITION. Includes a full range of treasure hunting methods from research techniques to detector operation, from legality to gold dredging. Don't worry that this material overlaps THM #6 ... both of Karl's MANUALS are 100% different from each other but yet are crammed with information you should know about treasure hunting. Illustrated. 334 pages.

SUCCESSFUL COIN HUNTING. Charles Garrett. Ram Publishing Company. The best and most complete guide to successful coin hunting, this book explains fully the how's, where's, and when's of searching for coins and related objects. It also includes a complete explanation of how to select and use the various types of coin hunting metal detectors. Based on more than twenty years of actual in-the-field experience by the author, this volume contains a great amount of practical coin hunting information that will not be found elsewhere. Profusely illustrated with over 100 photographs. 248 pages.

TREASURE HUNTING PAYS OFF! Charles Garrett. Ram Publishing Company. This book will give you an excellent introduction to all facets of treasure hunting. It tells you how to begin and be successful in general treasure hunting; coin hunting; relic, cache, and bottle seeking; and prospecting. It describes the various kinds of metal/mineral detectors and tells you how to go about selecting the correct type for all kinds of searching. This is an excellent guidebook for the beginner, but yet contains tips and ideas for the experienced TH'er. Illustrated. 92 pages.

PROFESSIONAL TREASURE HUNTER. George Mroczkowski. Ram Publishing Company. Research is 90 percent of the success of any treasure hunting endeavor. You will become a better treasure hunter by learning how, through proper treasure hunting techniques and methods, George was able to find treasure sites, obtain permission to search (even from the U. S. Government), select and use the proper equipment, and then recover treasure in many instances. If treasure was not found, valuable clues and historical artifacts were located that made it worthwhile or kept the search alive. Profusely illustrated. 154 pages.

BOOK ORDER BLANK

See your detector dealer or bookstore or send check or money order directly to Ram for prompt, postage paid shipping. If not completely satisfied return book(s) within 10 days for a full refund.

_____MODERN METAL DETECTORS $9.95
_____DETECTOR OWNER'S MANUAL $8.95
_____ELECTRONIC PROSPECTING $4.95
_____GOLD PANNING IS EASY $6.95
_____COMPLETE VLF-TR METAL
     DETECTOR HANDBOOK (THE) (ALL
     ABOUT GROUND CANCELING
     METAL DETECTORS) $8.95

_____ROBERT MARX. QUEST FOR
     TREASURE $11.95
_____TREASURE HUNTER'S MANUAL #6 $9.95
_____TREASURE HUNTER'S MANUAL #7 $9.95
_____SUCCESSFUL COIN HUNTING $8.95
_____TREASURE HUNTING PAYS OFF. $4.95
_____PROFESSIONAL TREASURE
     HUNTER $7.95

Please add 50¢ for each book ordered (to a maximum of $2) for handling charges.

Total for Items	$ _____
Texas Residents Add 7 1/4% State Tax	_____
Handling Charge	_____
Total of Above	$ _____

ENCLOSED IS MY CHECK OR MONEY ORDER $ _____

I prefer to purchase through my MasterCard (   ) or Visa (   ) account. (Check one.)

_____   _____
Card Number   Bank Identifier Number

_____   _____
Expiration Date   Signature (Order must be signed.)

NAME _____

ADDRESS _____

CITY _____

STATE _____ ZIP _____

PLACE MY NAME ON YOUR MAILING LIST ☐

Ram Publishing Company
P.O. Drawer 38649, Dallas, Texas 75238

Dept. SC18
214-278-8439
DEALER INQUIRIES WELCOME

207

NOTES

NOTES

NOTES